Maidstone M

A 1950's childhoc

Julia Botterell

First Published in Great Britain
as a paperback original

By Julia Botterell 2010

other books by this author
Denbigh Lacquer
2009

ISBN 978-0-9563647-1-5

Printed and bound in Great Britain by
Think Ink
11-13 Philip Road, Ipswich,
Suffolk IP2 8BH

A brief note about the author

After finishing a three year teachers training course in Bingley, in the West Riding of Yorkshire Julia married and went back to her home county Kent to teach at a small primary school in Goudhurst before moving to North Wales in 1974.
She taught at an infant school in Mynydd Isa for ten years before taking up a deputy headship in Wrexham. She finally became a head teacher, remaining at the school for twenty one years until her retirement in 2005.
In 2009 she completed her first book, *Denbigh Lacquer*.
Her interests include cooking for friends, travelling, cats, wildlife, gardens, the theatre, researching Family History and reading.

Maidstone Maid
A 1950's childhood in Kent

Foreword

Looking back I have found that the articles and accounts of the 1950's and the swinging permissive 1960's strangely bear little relation to the times that I remembered when growing up on a large council estate in on the outskirts of Maidstone in Kent. My mundane, working class childhood definitely reflected the more austere days of the 1940's. Perhaps it was the city dwellers who set the trend and we just never managed to catch up.

Our week was defined by duties and chores. We went to church on Sunday and had a mid-day 'roast dinner'. Monday was washday; taking over the entire morning or longer if it happened to rain, followed by Shepherds pie or something cold left over from the Sunday's roast. Tuesdays were devoted to dreary grocery shopping in town and most Saturday afternoons were spent along at Gran's house dutifully completing her list of chores once we had queued up outside the council office that morning to pay the rent.

We 'council kids' were scornfully defined by the sprawling estate on which we lived, and our woeful lack of money did much to temper to our aspirations. Throughout my early years it caused me embarrassment, bewildering shame and much later, as a teenager, burning resentment to be judged as merely a product of that estate.

From around the age of seven, the natural beautiful Mote Park, just on our doorstep, and the Bluebell Woods in Willington Street, became our treasured playgrounds where we could joyously lose ourselves and let our imaginations run riotously free.

Later on it was the inspirational teachers at Senacre Secondary School, in Sutton Road, who taught us to believe in ourselves and in so doing allowed us to consider a different future than as a shop assistant at Woolworths or a factory worker at Sharps Toffee.

At home we didn't lock our doors, not because we didn't think that there were burglars about but we felt that we had nothing of value for them to steal. Most Mums that I knew stayed at home and looked after their children with their family or in-laws living just a few streets away. Mum's chatted on the bus going to town; waiting at the bus stop, and over the back garden fences whilst hanging out the washing but no real intimacy was formed or first names used and we certainly didn't go in for invites to coffee mornings. Dads remained strangers disappearing for work each morning and not arriving home on their bikes until quite late.

We had no supermarkets with exotic foreign foods, or self-service shops in which to forage. Shop assistants brought the appropriate item from under the counter or scaled the wall on a flimsy ladder to fetch down the correct shoe box. The corner shop sold broken biscuits from tins placed on the floor in front of the counter which were sold by weight on brass scales. The shop assistant jotted down the prices on a scrap of paper before we requested the next item, then totalling the pounds, shillings and pence amount with a stubby pencil that had been securely lodged behind his ear.

As we saw few advertisements, we didn't feel the need to try out a new product. We used what had been tried and tested by the previous generation and kept every piece of string, sealing wax, wrapping paper, stray buttons and paperclips 'just in case' until we had overflowing jars of useless scraps scattered around the house. Socks were darned, hems lowered or shortened according to fashion or need and we prided ourselves on 'making things last'. Foods did not have 'sell by' dates or 'best before' dates, we used our sense of smell and sight to assess its merits to be fit for human consumption.

Being greedy or taking 'more than your fair share' could result in achromous resentment although our Dad despaired when he heard us quarrelling over which was the' biggest half.

"There is no such thing as a 'bigger' half", he unfailingly tried to educate us and we would be temporally quietened until he was out of earshot before the whispered argument resumed.

We had no concept of being politically correct assuming that everyone had the right to 'speak their mind' and a duty to be fair.

Living 'on tick' or credit wasn't an available option for us so much time was spent having to save up for a desired item or for the ominous 'rainy day' eventuality. To be in debt would have brought terrible shame on a family and so we 'cut our cloth' accordingly for once there was no money left in Mum's purse we would just have to wait until Dad's Friday's wage packet arrived.

For the children of today's generation all this must seem quite Dickensian. They run up debts of hundreds and in some cases thousands of pounds without a qualm, paying off just the minimum on each credit card or extending their overdraft. For my generation such profligacy seems indecent at best and quite criminal when a declaration of bankruptcy is considered to be a legitimate option.

When we had family outings to the coast or had enjoyed a picnic in the park we dutifully packed away our rubbish to take back home with us, as did everyone whom we knew. Only very common people swore in public, spat in the gutter or ate food in the street.

So were they the good old days? Perhaps in some ways they were but I certainly wouldn't want to go back. Nostalgic for some of the moments of childhood, the magic of Christmas; believing in fairies for Tinkerbelle's sake and rushing headlong through the snow on a sledge with Dad sitting behind? Yes they were certainly wonderful but they rightly belong in the past.

Acknowledgements

Throughout the last few months I have prodded Mum into remembering names, dates and places that I could only faintly recall, only for her to come up with some unexpected details which have triggered off other memories for me. And then I have used photographs, old ration books, magazine and newspaper cuttings and other paraphernalia that would have been thrown away in most households, which she had kept safely tucked away in cupboards and drawers. Had it not been stored away I would not have been able to have used the information. So much for all the years teasing her about her squirrel mentality; so thanks Mum for that!

Thanks to my sister Heather for confirming some details when I became a little hazy on the sequence of events or the names of places and people, and to Stephanie for providing a couple of old photographs when we were at school together.

I need to thank Maureen Parker, my fellow WI Book Club enthusiast, for proof reading and correcting the manuscript. Finally thanks to my Al for his patience and constant encouragement whilst I have been engaged in this enterprise.

Chapter 1   1950 -1957 Infant days

I came into the world just nine days after the new decade of 1950 began.

The year 1950 finally signalled the end of the 2nd World War years of the 1940's but still carried the legacy of austerity and deprivation wrought by the crippling debt the country had to repay. Before I was six months old, the Korean War called upon my Dad to once again be away from home serving with the 'wavy navy' for the next two years from 1950 until 1952. His employers at Hayle Paper Mill, Maidstone, Jack and Remy Green, wrote to tell him that they were very sorry to lose him due to,

'the Present Emergency after such a short time with us and hope that the absence is brief and that you will come back to us as soon as possible........your cheerful face and excellent work will be missed but from the national point of view we are glad that there are some chaps like you who are ready to do that when the situation arises.......we have a small present to speed you on your way ...please tell your wife that if she has any worries or troubles to come and see us'.

My birth in January, at Maidstone Hospital, however, had been a cause for celebration, as it ensured the acquisition of an eagerly awaited three bed-roomed semi-detached council house on the newly created Shepway Estate in Maidstone. A criterion of points, devised by the council, required a married couple to have at least two children. Finally Mum and Dad were able to set up home together after six years of marriage that had survived a war and sharing a house with Mum's parents and her younger sister Betty, in the better off, private end of Plains Avenue. Dad had been employed by an electrical company Oswald Jones in Maidstone for two years whilst they were living there, after leaving the Royal Navy, from 1946 until 1948.

The well-positioned house on Oxford Road overlooked the natural parkland of Mote Park. When Dad had been courting Mum there had been a herd of deer, but by the time I arrived sheep and cows were enjoying the lush grass amongst the clumps of willowy stinging nettles and spotted dock leaves, as they meandered and munched their way through the unspoilt park. The land, previously known as Shepherd's Way according to the 1821 Greenwood Map of Maidstone, upon which our house was built had supported a soft fruit farm. Sandy soil and large clumps of crumbly white chalk had been exposed as an estate of council buildings took shape, with black berry brambles still clinging on tenaciously to the land. Our house was built on a layer of solid rock which Dad used to good landscaping effect once they had settled in.

I watched the late afternoon sunshine casting shafts of light across the landing as I lay in my pram at the bottom of the stairs. Was this possible? Could I have remembered such a thing? Mum had verified that she had indeed parked the large pram in the hall, with me facing up the stairs, but could a tiny child recall such an early experience? But still I imagine that I remember contentment, warmth, and happiness staring in wonder and delight as the soft fading light moved westwards.

The Ideal Home Exhibition of 1951 had asked the Women's Institute for some ideas on what they thought constituted an Ideal Home. They had verified that it should have a hall big enough to accommodate a pram ,an outhouse with a fuel store, laundry room, toilet and space to store garden tools and that there should be somewhere to store 'muddy boots'.. They had agreed that the kitchen should have a larder and that the 'parlour' should be heated with an open fire whilst upstairs there would be 'heated radiators for the bedrooms', (according to the WI Honorary Archivist Anne Stamper)

New mums, in those early Welfare State days, pushed along their babies in their large unwieldy prams to the clinic for their babies to be checked, weighed and to receive concentrated orange juice and cod

2

liver oil. It wasn't long before Mum found that the orange juice was too acidic for me as I came out in a livid red rash. But I can still taste the spoonfuls of cod lover oil and thick syrupy brown malt extract that we were given with strict instructions to 'lick the spoon clean'.

In those first few years Dad, excited by the novelty of having a place of their own, heaved and positioned the thick slabs of rock that he had uncovered from a thin covering of soil into place. In the front garden he fashioned a rockery, surrounded it with stepping stones and then used more substantial rocks to upend and place around the edges to create a sunken garden. A rough dry stone wall completed the final area towards the fence. On the other side of the pathway he designed a top lawn with an arbour of supported roses; another dry stone wall with two smaller steps finally completed that side. As our plot of land resembled a triangle it meant that the back garden disappeared into a tiny point and the front garden opened wide onto the pavement. Still he was invigorated with enthusiasm in those early years and the small back garden was planted with cabbages, runner beans and peas. A small grass seeded area at the back of the house attempted to resemble a lawn and another little rockery denoted the separation of the vegetable patch and the patchy lawn. He erected two tall poles to support a washing line and finally set up his lathe and machinery in the separate garden shed which also accommodated a separate outside toilet and, facing towards the house, a two sectioned coal bunker, one side for coal and one for coke and a hook for the tin bath.

I remember illicitly sampling the sweet tasting peas stolen before they were able to fatten up. In some pods a tiny worm would slither from hole bored into the pea and the worm's deposits would stick to the adjoining pea. I recall swinging on the wooden side gate, beside the tall yellow and orange flowers that were besieged by hungry bees, watching forlornly as school children routinely hurried to and from school, fervently wishing I could be free to join them. Perhaps I could have climbed over and danced down the path towards them but I didn't. Standing on the bottom rung, scraping the toe of my dusty sandal on the bars I impatiently waited for my fifth birthday to arrive.

3

Whilst the house was well built it was soon apparent that there were some glaring faults within. The stubborn kitchen coke-fired boiler routinely refused to keep alight. It was the only means by which we could heat the water but either the dusty coke doused the flames or the wind changed direction and sent billowing smoke into the kitchen. It frazzled my exasperated Mum. More than once we would be told that there was no hot water to be had and so the electric copper kettle expensively boiled the required small amount for emergencies.

And we rarely used the north facing front room. This had to be heated by the sulky coal fire. Dad would coax it with small pieces of wood, scrunched up newspaper and a few plump pieces of well chosen jet-black coal. He would light different sections of the paper and we would watch hopefully as the small flames licked around the edges, smouldering the wood, before their final flicker of death. More paper and wood would be assembled and as the wood took hold Dad would stretch out a sheet of newspaper to draw the fire. The Daily Mirror would glow yellow; we would hear the ominous rage of fire before he ceremoniously whipped away the scorched newsprint. As sides of the fireplace glistened and glowed the tiny flames finally died away leaving us left with just a fallen pile of dusty coal.

The whole performance would begin again with fire lighters added to the pyramid of kindling. A large piece of cardboard would replace the sheet of newspaper and I would watch with trepidation as the roar of fire travelled up the chimney threatening to set the house alight. Just as the cardboard began to darken Dad would snatch it away and we would be engulfed in smoke before realising that the coals were glowing and the fire was finally alight. Every so often it would remind us of its spiteful presence by spitting out hot cinders leaving black holes and singe marks on the half moon rug.

The uncarpeted room was sparsely furnished with two square uncomfortable armchairs, a small bookcase, and an upright piano manufactured by Henry Ward of 100 Great Russell Street, Bloomsbury, London and sold, according to the gold crested label depicting the lion and a unicorn, by Stephen French, a Pianoforte and

4

Music Warehouse, at 60 The High Street (next to the Post Office) Maidstone.

We spent our time in the warmer dining room. In the evenings Mum would clatter in the kitchen and Dad would disappear into his shed to work on his loco unless the weather was bitter and his little heater could not warm him.

When I was still sleeping in a cot I was placed by the window in Mum and Dad's bedroom in the front, but once I was ready for my own bed I was given the little north-west facing bedroom. It rarely saw the sun's rays even on the hottest summer's day. In the winter the curtain would stick to the leaf-printed frosted window. Water collected on the window sill and thin bands of ice lined the metal frames. My bedding would become heavier as extra blankets and coats were piled on to exclude the cold. A smelly paraffin heater was commissioned to heat the room but when all attempts at keeping me warm failed I would be sent to share my sister Heather's double bed in the back south-east facing bedroom. Inevitable, despite all dire warnings to behave, we would end up fighting over the hot water bottle and how much space in the bed each was occupying.

"This is my side!" Heather banged her hand down on the middle of the bed to emphasis her point, just missing my legs.

"No this is the middle!" I retaliated, trying to gain a few extra inches whilst attempting to secure the hot water bottle with my toes.

Sometimes the paraffin heater and a mountain of coats and blankets piled on me seemed a better, more peaceful option for my harassed parents. Getting dressed or undressed involved a complicated process of removing pyjamas whilst still under the covers and easing on knickers, vests, and a liberty bodice that had been kept warm inside the bed, then pulling on a jumper and skirt before finally emerging from the bed. The reverse took place at night with the day clothes kept just under the eiderdown. On mornings when it was even too cold to stay upstairs to get dressed we would come down to the dining room and change in front of the new rectangular paraffin heater. Mum would waft our clothes in front of it trying to air them and warm them a little. I happened to stand too close to the heater and suddenly found that I had burnt myself on the top vented grill. Mum inspected the damage. I had red weals striped across my buttocks. When Dad heard about it all he could do was laugh.

For years afterwards he would often wink and say, "and how's stripes today?" Knowing that I would be mortified if anyone knew what he meant.

Dad also provided a daily amusement for me as he always used the kitchen sink for his morning wash and shave. Somehow I never thought to question why it was that he washed there whereas we washed upstairs in the bathroom. Perhaps it was a legacy from his upbringing in Nottingham where the miners used the kitchen sink or tub in the scullery. As he stripped down to his vest, his braces dangling by the sides of his trousers I would watch in fascination as he lathered his face with his favourite Imperial Leather shaving soap and then proceed to scrap clean lines through the foam exposing his slightly reddened skin underneath. The process would finish with a splash of aftershave making his face tingle.

"Just the job!" but he would involuntarily shiver with the sting.

On one shoulder he had a gash of jagged skin, the result of a burn that he had sustained in the engine room during his days at sea in the war. He had been carrying a very hot piece of machinery on his shoulder, which he had inadequately padded with some cloth, but the cloth had slipped away and exposed his flesh to the searing heat. We called it his 'war wound'. He always felt the cold and rarely took off his pullover. On very hot days he would finally roll up his sleeves, turning them carefully until his arm was exposed just above the elbow. When he stripped to wash his white skin ended just at that point. Although he hated the cold weather he had equally hated the sand and the heat of the Middle East, when stationed in Alexandra. And so the only parts that ever saw the sun even on the hottest days, was the top of his head, his face and his lower arms. I watched him clip the white and gold collar stud on to the back of the stiff starched collar to his shirt and then turn it down in half to rest against his neck. Once the collar had become grey on one side he would turn the collar inside-out hiding the grimy part inside.

Just as the house was absurdly cold in the winter so it could be unbearably hot for Mum working in the kitchen during the summer months. She had no refrigerator so our fresh meat was suspended in a metal box meat safe in the hall; this being the coolest place in the house. The squat coke fired boiler, positioned in the corner of the kitchen still had to remain alight to provide hot water, and so Mum would have the back door wide open attempting to cool herself as she baked cakes or kneaded the pastry for her steak and kidney pies, weighing out the flour and margarine and lard on her green metal kitchen scales; flour in one side and the weights resting on the opposite tray. Milk would 'go off', butter turn rancid as the heat took effect and my boredom at being at home, too young to be at school, meant that she had the added frustration of suggesting activities that would engage me whilst she wrestled with sticky pastry. She favoured making flaky pastry, mixing the flour with water then rolling it out and spreading dotted dollops of white lard and 'marg' across the expanse of pastry. She carefully folded one third towards the middle and then the other third across, before rolling it out thinly. The procedure would be repeated with more applications of lard and margarine until she had used up the allotted amount of fats. Copious amounts of flour spread over the white metal pastry board and onto the floor, yet despite the chaotic method her pastry was always light and papery. Sometimes I was allowed back into the kitchen. Mum would let me through the child-gate that was tightly wedged between the dining room and where she was working in the kitchen. I would shape the trimmings of the pastry using a little green clown-man shaped cutter. Pale creamy pastry turned sludgy grey-brown under my fingers as I attempted to roll, cut and place the irregular little men on the baking tray.

On days when Mum was not too busy she would sit at the dining room table and I would stand on a little stool combing her hair until the soporific effect finally caused her to fall asleep.

I have suddenly remembered! An old Belfast sink in the kitchen with its bleached scrubbed wooden draining board where I sat waiting to be bathed as a small infant; my feet dangling in the non too warm water. I asked for my singing bird which was kept on the window sill. The blue plastic bird would be half filled with water and as I blew through the tail-end spout he would warble and sing to me. I loved his nightingale song; asking for him to be refilled and to coax his chirruping until the tepid water in the sink turned quite cold. Standing up in the sink as the soap stained scummy grey water swirled down plughole Mum would rub me vigorously and then lifting me, towel wrapped and warm, down onto the cold kitchen floor. How old could I have been then? Perhaps two or three? I was old enough to know not to suck but to blow the singing bird into performing his song, but young enough to make the occasional mistake spluttering out soapy water before attempting another go.

I must have been a little taller then when able to stand on the wooden three legged stool and play with the pots and pans in the sink, endlessly amused by the action of filling, pouring and emptying them in the bubbly water. Another memory has just leapt into my mind. I am using extra washing-up liquid, shaping my thumb and index finger to form a circle and then scooping the rich soapy water across the hole and gently blowing onto the membrane to form bubbles. Fascinated I watch the languid heavy rainbow bubbles drift down to the floor, plopping on contact with the lino.

What other amusements did I have whilst impatiently waiting to go to school and to acquire a myriad of friends? Perhaps we had allowed the stray 'cee ay tee' black cat to join our household by then. I know that my neighbour's child and I used to catch their tabby cat and attempt to dress him in a bonnet and dress before tucking him under a cot blanket and wheeling him around in a pram. I have the black and white photograph of us both, slightly grubby looking toddlers, me with an ineffectual ribbon bow tied into my straight straggly hair; and her with enviable tousled curls, both of us attempting to keep the cat down in the pram before he seized his chance to rid himself of both bonnet and pram and rush off down the garden path escaping from us until the next time that we caught him. He must have been a very good natured cat not to have scratched us for tormenting him.

Confined to the back garden by the side gate I could just catch a glimpse of the Rag and Bone man with his cart and balloons as his haunting drawn-out cry attracted 'stay at home' mums and children to him. I wanted to go out and see what he would have, but we never seemed to have any old clothes to give him. I fretted as his horse, cart and cry disappeared, leaving me with just a tantalising echo, "raaahgg n boawne, raaahgg n boawne" trailing after him.

I have just remembered again. A little bottle filled with water, containing a deep sea diver wearing a globe-like helmet and big boots. His task was to reach the treasure chest at the bottom of the bottle but nearby lurked an octopus that he had to evade during his quest. I think that we pressed a red rubber top on the bottle and that would send him sinking down. I wonder what happened to it. It kept us amused for ages as we sat on the kitchen step vying to have a turn to send the diver down.

"My turn now, he touched the octopus."

"No he didn't!"

"I saw it move."

"Don't snatch, I'll tell Mum."

"It's not fair!"

In those formal,' Mr and Mrs' days, our neighbours kept themselves very much to themselves. Our immediate 'back door facing back door' neighbour rarely spoke except to pass a mundane comment about the weather. Strangely enough this austere Mr Cummings was chosen to be my Godfather and then proceeded to ignore me and not engage in conversation with my parents either. I would watch him from a safe distance, being somewhat afraid of him, as he mechanically stirred his cup of tea round and round whilst sitting on the back door step.

The choking 'pea soup' smog of 1952 meant that we could hardly see the swirling grey green daylight from morning to dusk and the cold winters made shopping a chore for Mum in her thin mustard yellow winter coat. People would suddenly appear as ghostly presences from nowhere and then disappear, swallowed into the thick fog. The nearest shop 'Skinners' was a good mile away on Plains Avenue Mum would take her shopping bag and pile the rest of the goods on the

9

pram. Taking the bus to town was impossible with me and the bulky pram so she had to pay the inflated prices set by that Skinners. Eventually she arranged for a small box of groceries to be delivered each Tuesday to lessen the numbers of trips out, but we always seemed to run out of some essential item so another forage would be made necessary.

Cold winters and the miserable wet summers kept me housebound and isolated since my sister, being five years older, was at school during the week days. Even at weekends her activities and interests excluded me. I hankered to be outside, she enjoyed her painting and sewing, I was a nuisance. We succumbed to numerous coughs and colds. Not having tissues and very few hankies Mum resorted to tearing up rags which then had to be boiled for use again. My cardigan cuff would become distorted as I attempted to stuff a sodden green snotty rag up my damp woolly sleeve.

My lonely time spent indoors was somewhat relieved by listening to the wireless in the dining room, after dinner when Daphne Oxenford read me stories on the Light programme's 'Listen with Mother'.

"Are you sitting comfortably? Then I'll begin."

I joined in with all the Nursery Rhymes until I was word perfect;

'See saw, Margery Daw,

Jackie will have a new master,

He will have but a penny a day,

Because he can't go any faster.'

We had an old farm yard board with a red roofed farmer's house, detachable wooden cow sheds, stables for the horses, green lead fences that could be linked together to make small fields and a pig pen. The old farmer and his wife, carrying a bucket, were rough lead models that refused to stand up due to bent and uneven legs. Our lead animals followed suit; some had legs that had buckled with age and others had missing legs which meant that they had to be propped against another animal to stay upright. Dad teased Heather calling them 'anomalies' instead of animals. Our farm boasted a few hens, some ducks, two or three black and pink pigs, dented black and white cows, a couple of horses and some sheep some fashioned to stand precariously on their wobbly legs, whilst others were safer in a lying down position. We put the horse to stand in their stables watching out for the farmers wife, the pigs lined up at the piggery side by side, some sheep were allowed to wander around a fenced field segregated from the Friesians, whilst the hens and ducks flocked together around the farmyard pond which was a piece of mirror set into the green painted board. All of the animals had seen better days, some boasted of their time with Noah, but to us they were precious; to be carefully tended.

At night my 'comfort' was a thin piece of material that I would lightly rub across my lips. It gave me exquisite happiness that was painfully jarred when Mum decided that the material had become far too grubby. She surreptitiously washed it and I was handed back the harsh strange smelling comforter. I cried at the betrayal, refusing to accept it until finally driven to have something to aid my sleep. The bad dreams hadn't started then, or if they had then I can't recall the horrors that made me fearful of the dark, of shadows and the unexplained sounds of night.

I was still too young to enjoy the pleasures of playing all day in Mote Park; all that was still to come. My horizons were confined to our house, the back garden, glimpses of the road from the side gate, accompanied trips to the shops, the town, and visits to 49 Plains Avenue.

For my sister Heather, this, our Grandmother's house, represented her emotional home. She had spent her first five years with both grandparents; forging a strong bond with them both whilst my Dad was away in the Royal Navy. Mum and her younger sister Betty lived together in the solid three bed roomed semi at the end of Plains Avenue. Mum's friend, Joan, also lived further along the road towards Loose Road. My grandfather, Will, was an easy going man. He could turn his hand to most things. They kept chickens at the bottom of the garden to supplement the war rations and a large healthy vegetable and fruit plot kept them well supplied. In the back garden Will had dug a small pond stocked with a few goldfish. An apple and pear tree overshadowed the area. Some plump red dessert and ordinary green furry gooseberry bushes with particularly savage prickles had been planted by the shed. In the spring a riot of Lily of the Valley invaded the lawn; managing to grow through the concreted pathway and spread themselves in a lush white and green carpet under the fruit bushes and trees.

Will, well loved and very close to his daughter Joyce, made and repaired toys for his granddaughter Heather. Dorothy kept a tidy well ordered house; she had worked as a domestic servant in a large house in London during her youth and had not only learnt skills in housekeeping but had also been trained to help the cook in the busy kitchen. She carefully managed the war rations so the family ate moderately well. As the family kept chickens at the bottom of the garden they received chicken feed in place of the allotted 'one egg per person' a week according to the dictates of Lord Woolton, head of the Ministry of Food. Concocting pies and stews, puddings and tarts from the family-pooled rations of three ounces of cheese per person and two ounces of fats, she also accommodated a little lad from the East End of London who was housed with them for a short while, even buying him new shoes from Marks and Spencer at the cost of 15/- which came from her own purse. One morning as she busied herself in the kitchen he wandered in, wide-eyed, watching the hustle and bustle of her cooking.

Finally he couldn't help himself. "Aint yer got a lot of saucepans missis?"

Startled Dorothy said "Well yes, we need them for our dinner, why, doesn't your Mum cook?"

"Narrh, me Mum gets us fish 'n chips and ven goes off to the flicks."

Apparently he went back home soon afterwards as he had contracted a nasty dose of Impetigo and Gran refused to have him back.

My Granddad's sudden death out in the street by South Park in May 1949 caused great distress in the household, overshadowing Mum's delight in her second pregnancy. A post mortem was held investigating the nature of his death. Will had been a valued and well liked mechanic at Roots Garage, Mill Street, situated in the middle of

Maidstone. Mum remembered that their clients often asked if Will Kempshall would be doing the work for them.

"They knew that he would always do a good job."

During the beginning of the 1st World War he had been invalided out of the army, due to suffering from a severe kick from one of the horses that he was caring for, and the injury had caused him constant pain from then on. The coroner, at the inquest, criticised the doctor who had prescribed a 'vigorous walk and some fresh air' despite Will being in very poor health. Will subsequently collapsed and died from pleurisy. Dorothy's shock at losing her beloved Will brought with it a profound depression that overshadowed the rest of her life. Her relationship with Mum had not been an easy one. She could not share Mum's happiness in securing a house of her own and probably was saddened to lose the daily contact with Heather although Betty, her younger daughter was still living at home.

Dorothy watched as Joyce plaited Heather's long light brown hair. The child squirmed restlessly on the chair becoming irritated at sitting so long.

"Hold still Heather!"

If only she was more deft at the task. She could have done it in half the time; Joyce was always so clumsy at these things.

"Shall I finish her?"

Joyce frowned, "no I've almost done now." Why did she always have to interfere? She spoilt Heather, making her difficult to handle, and then blamed her for not being able to control her own child. Heather and her stubborn ways; goodness knows where she got it from.

Well, thought Dorothy, when you move out and have no one to help, and with another child to care for, you'll soon see on which side your bread was buttered and no mistake. Always making things difficult; wanting to do things your way. She might look a thin scrap of nothing but she would dig her heels in and then there would be no helping her. And Will and I provided a roof over their heads when they had nothing.Will even gave Amos money for the wedding ring because he was so foolish with money, goodness knows what he spend his money on in the Navy, it wasn't as if he drank, and this is the way we get treated. We could have asked for more when she was with the WRENS but no, her father was too soft on her and now she'll find out what it is like to fend for themselves. But then their life was just beginning and her life was over now.

She pressed her lips together and went into the kitchen to make a cup of tea. Let her get on with it then. There will be tears before too long no doubt.

Joyce watched the aproned figure walk into the kitchen. Pulling the strands of hair into the final plait before tying the ribbon into a bow she allowed Heather to wrestle away.

"I hate my hair." Heather couldn't resist a parting shot. "When I grow up I shall cut it all off!"

"When you grow up you can!" Joyce's pink cheeks betrayed her frustration. "And I shall tell your father what a naughty girl you have been for me."

She watched her little daughter flounce into the kitchen. And I bet Mum gives her a biscuit even 'tho she knows that she has been rude, she thought to herself. How will I ever manage her when she has been so spoilt? And I've heard her whispering, when she didn't know that I could hear, 'you can call me Mum,' she said to her. I should have had it out with her there and then, but with Dad being so ill and then everything happening. Oh I don't know. I shall be glad to get out.

I knew from an early age that Gran was not easy with me. Perhaps I resembled Joyce and that's why she was indifferent at best and at other times quite cold. I never felt comfortable with her. I didn't like the dark house. Somehow it frightened me. The back room, which seemed to be both the dining room and front room combined, looked out onto the pretty back garden. The two recesses either side of the fire place had enclosed cupboards; the sludgy brown paint was streaked to resemble wood grain. At the door a thick curtain was suspended on a metal rod to prevent draughts. A small television with a tiny screen would eventually, in later years, sit on a cupboard in one corner whilst a dark oak sideboard, table and four chairs attempted to fit into the rest of the space. As I sat alone in the room the door curtain would billow without warning towards me or the hem would

14

quiver imperceptivity. I would be so afraid my throat would shrink so much that I couldn't even cry out. The door thing knew that I was afraid. One day it would take me. I could not bear to be alone in any part of the house. The downstairs toilet situated just outside the kitchen next to the coal store, held terrors of its own. A tiny lamp bulb, no bigger than the nail on my little finger, was held onto the wall by a single nail just lighting one small corner of the ceiling. The rest of the area was dark even when the daylight was bright outside. A roll of thin, hard, shiny Izal toilet paper hung from a nail. I imagined long legged spiders creeping and scuttling towards me and then returning to their thick webs in the recesses of the walls. There was no inside toilet just an enamel bath upstairs overhung with an old metal gas fired geezer that would explode into life, its blue flames threatening to escape from within. The basin held a single piece of smelly green carbolic soap.

I was pleased to be back into the safety of our own house. The chaos and untidiness endeared itself to me after a visit to 49.

Sometimes we would visit Skinners grocery shop on the way home and buy broken biscuits from the tin boxes situated on the floor in front of the counter. Mr Skinner had a bacon slicer and more often than not he would be found behind the counter slicing thin rashers. I watched with horrid fascination as the steel wheel slid through the meat and then as he wrapped the rashers in greaseproof paper, slightly clumsily, due to having lost most of his fingers on one hand. The stumps were bulbous and pink. I can't remember how he lost these fingers but always imagined that it had been due to the bacon slicer. I dare not look at the glistening sausages grouped together in the glass fronted cabinet queasily resembling his short finger stumps.

Finally the day arrived when I was able to go to school; a term after my fifth birthday. The infant school, now a Red Cross Centre, in School Lane had just two classrooms that were separated by a huge concertina set of doors that were pulled back to create one room on special occasions. The high windows ensured a well lit room but no view to the outside world. In each classroom sat a black iron cast

15

stove. In the 'baby room' was a wooden rocking horse but the neighbouring class room had desks and chairs more suitable for serious study. On a pupil's birthday the doors would be pulled back and all infants would sit together and watch as Kelpie, the gentle giant boxer dog, owned by the head teacher, would sit and sing/howl its version of 'Happy Birthday'. I would be entranced by the performance. A small trinket musical box would then be opened and a tiny ballerina would twirl to the tune. In one little compartment the fortunate birthday child would be able to retrieve a sweet after the dance had finished. It was a wonder, an absolute delight that completely captivated my imagination. The ballerina lived in that box. She came alive just for a few moments and I knew that she was real. I loved my days in school. I played alongside the other infants often quite oblivious of them. I was in a world of my own for the first year. Activities of card making and painting absorbed me. Modelling lumps of brown clay into animal shapes delighted me. Manufacturing Christmas elves from pine cones and pipe cleaners, with a hat fashioned from an acorn cup, allowed me to show off my accomplishments to my parents. My mind was stimulated by the variety of tasks set before me. In empty egg shells we planted mustard and cress seeds sprinkling them on damp cotton wool. They were placed on the high window ledges out of harm's way until finally the tiny green leafy shoots peeped through. They graced the nature table, after we drew a face on our shell, before taking them home in time for Easter. We cut out sticky paper to create Mother's Day cards and neatly copied a message inside. The Happy Venture Dick and Dora books fascinated me and I loved the red and blue detailed drawings. I don't remember learning to read but can recall the thrill of being able to hear the words in my head without sounding them out. It suddenly became a wonderful intimate private relationship.

One day sitting on the stairs at home I heard my Mum say 'where is that cee ay tee' and realised that although I knew that she was referring to our cat she was actually spelling out the letters C A T, why had I never realised that before!

Nature trips and collecting bits and pieces for the nature table constantly appealed to me. We had one trip forming the inevitable two by two crocodile walk into Mote Park, which was merely a few minutes walk away from the school. Detailed to collect leaves of different shapes and sizes for the nature table or to create some sort of collage on our return, I had happily collected a handful only to be approached by a particularly bold sheep who decided that my leaves looked most appealing and quickly snatched them from me. Dejectedly I returned to school empty handed. Did that really happen or did I just drop them on the way back?

As I had an older sister and we had little money so I regularly became a 'second hand rose' wearing hand-me-downs that Heather had outgrown. I angrily wished that I had had an older brother instead of a sister, desperately wanting new clothes of my own. One day my wish was granted. It must have been a party day at the school; as for once I wore a new pink dress. The shiny material had matt pink dots and at the waist was a large sash that tied at the back. I was in seventh heaven spinning around to make the hem swirl and billow. Mum must have decided that it would be a good idea to curl my lank thin hair like Shirley Temple. Unfortunately any resemblance of that child star stayed in her mind's eye as the photograph of me taken at that time demonstrated.

In Heather's wardrobe at home I had found a pair of Mum's shoes that she must have bought for her wedding. Strappy, with high heels, their silver–grey sparkle captivated me. When I was sure that no one was looking I slipped them on and tottered around the bedroom, feeling like a princess. Heather had been allowed to attend ballet and tap classes for a short time. Apparently she had been so naughty at the classes that Mum was asked to not take her again. I drew out the slightly scuffed pink shoes and tried them on, tying the pink ribbons around my ankles. Attempting to stand on tiptoe and making a few giddy turns I became a prima donna for a couple of seconds before losing balance and spoiling the effect. After falling in love with the wonderful shoes I pleaded with Mum to allow me to go to ballet school

17

but she was adamant. Heather had squared my pitch and there was nothing more to be said.

"I can't show my face there again. She kept running around the room. Such a naughty girl!"

And so my days at the infant school passed by. I made friends, played energetically on the small yard, learnt to skip and become a fast 'horse' pulling along the hapless 'cowboy' who had happened to lasso me until one day when I caused an accident by recklessly plunging around the playground at the end of the rope reins causing my 'cowboy' to lose his footing and bloody his nose on the unforgiving tarmac yard.

In the winter months we were allowed to place our frozen milk bottles next to the stove to warm it ready for drinking. We would watch as the milk tops still attached to the frozen milk would begin to settle back down onto the bottleneck. The only fly in the ointment to marr my happiness were the toilets. These were placed outside at the back, way across the yard. In the winter a pathway would be dug through the snow but even that adventure did not lessen my trepidation. Swaying spider webs laced the ceilings. Fat spiders, out of reach, sat waiting in the centre of their webs.

"Come into my parlour, said the spider to the fly."

I would do anything to avoid going in. Despite the pain of constipation accompanied by dizzy banging headaches I would attempt to blot out the need to 'go'. By the time I arrived home the stomach cramps would be unbearable but by then nature had been confounded and I needed medication. Spoonfuls of Liquid Paraffin were poured down my throat on a regular basis, Syrup of Figs would follow suit. At first I was nauseated by the foul taste but after so many years I almost got to like it, along with the equally shuddering liquid Malt Extract piled high and shiny, sticky, brown on a formidably large spoon.

Ugh, I still shudder at the memory.

And it did me no good. Ignoring the pleas of my body I just could not enter the school spider sanctum and so throughout my childhood and teenage years I was plagued by nauseous headaches and agonising stomach pains. The regime of not being able to go to the toilet until an

18

appointed playtime period, by which time my constitution had decided that it didn't want to 'play', wrecked my body's natural routine.

There were also some nasty remedies for boils. Gran would mix up a repellent grey poultice which had to be applied to the affected area once the poultice had been heated in a saucepan on her stove. This would 'draw out' the infection according to Gran. The pain of the burning muslin wrapped poultice simply increased the pain of the throbbing boil. I would attempt to squirm and twist as she firmly kept the hot poultice in place.

On a Saturday morning Gran would buy half a pint of cockles and whelks from the man who used to come round in his van. Watching her pick out the blob of fleshy jelly from each shell with a pin I was nauseated by them; they disgusted me. She enjoyed cooking and made brawn, steamed syrup puddings in a muslin bag, cooked tripe and steak and kidney puddings and taught me how to slice paper thin runner beans holding the bean horizontally between my finger and thumb. Not only very able in the kitchen she could also read music and play the piano and sew, using her old Singer Sewing machine with its bullet-shaped bobbin. Then she could crochet, read knitting patterns and even took time to teach me the rudiments of knitting, but I was always awkward under her watchful eye. I don't know why she did not pass on those skills to Mum who said that she was never allowed to help in the kitchen.

Still despite our uneasy relationship she made me knitted clothes for my dolls, carefully constructed bonnets tied with ribbon, booties similarly tied with ribbon, little dresses and matinee coats with pretty buttons.

Back at school although I loved my time there and revelled in all the activities I somehow did not listen to what was happening around me. Christmas concerts or special occasions always caught me out. Did I know that this was going to happen? Did I need a costume for the school concert or summer party? It was as if time stretched and shrank. I faintly would recall that someone did mention a fancy dress costume; that I was required to wear a bee costume for the play but somehow I always forgot to mention it to Mum. On fetching me from school she would find out from another parent about the impeding play, concert or party and then have to frantically sort something suitable out for me to wear. I was so often alone with my thoughts; muddling reality with my imagination. I did have friends but the relationships were often haphazard. I liked the idea of a 'best friend' but found it difficult to decide who that special person was. In my class we had a set of identical twins living just a few doors away from us. I could never understand why the teachers and other mothers constantly asked which one was which. To us children it was quite obvious which sister we were playing with or talking to; we just 'knew'. Rebellion had never been a strong feature in my early childhood. I can still remember the hurt look on Mum's face when I obeyed one of the twin's directions on leaving school to 'hide' from Mum as she came to fetch me. As we scampered past she watched in bewilderment as I disappeared into the twin's front garden.

One afternoon I went to a birthday party at a neighbour's house. After 'pass the parcel', 'kiss the postman' and 'musical chairs' we went into their dining room where a tea was laid out on the table. There were sandwiches, jelly and ice cream and a birthday cake decorated with little candles. I was keen to start on the lovely feast but knew that I needed to go to the toilet for a 'wee wee'. My embarrassment barred me from asking to leave the table. I wriggled and fidgeted hoping that it would pass, but the need to go became more and more pressing. Finally I my horror I could feel the plastic covered dining chair seat become warm and wet. Just as everyone rose from the table to leave the party their dog came snuffling towards me and began to lick the seat clean. Nobody ever mentioned the incident but even now I can remember the humiliating shame of the event.

Across the road from the school was the School Lane Post Office and red telephone box. As children we were exhorted to 'save for the future'. I had a Post Office savings account opened for me and each week I could buy a savings stamp to put into my book. This Post Office has long gone. A pub, 'The Century', was built on the site and then, a few years ago this was pulled down and the land acquired for housing.

Being naturally acquisitive children we often yanked open the heavy telephone box door and pressed button B to see if some distracted caller had forgotten to press the button after an aborted phone call and collect the pennies that clattered into the dish. And, if no one was looking, pretended to be making a phone call by inserting a finger into a numbered hole; turning the whirring dial round until it couldn't go any further. The heavy receiver clicked dutifully as we replaced it onto the cradle and pressing button B 'just in case'.

My second year at the infant school continued to engage me. Once again we planted mustard and cress seeds on blotting paper and cotton wool, wrote down our spellings and sums, my drawings and paintings were admired by my teacher and I glowed in the praise and the ease of my studies. I didn't find anything too hard until attempting to tell the time. Somehow the hands of the clock defeated me. I could use the clock for my multiplication tables but Time itself was obstinate; it mocked me. My Dad was also frustrated by my incomprehension. How could it be that a child who could add, subtract, divide and multiply could not tell the difference between the hour and minute hand? Half past five was the worst one to 'tell'. Was it half past six or half past five? I would attempt to guess and inevitably get it wrong. By now a black curtain of despair would descend as Dad held up his handmade cardboard clock face. Twirling the black hands around the face the inquisition would begin. 'What time is it?'

Guess, quickly before his voice hardens with annoyance! 'A quarter past three'.

'And now?'

'Ten to four.'

The answers were all correct perhaps it would stop.

'And this one?'

My heart thudded in my throat as I looked at the hands drawn down so close together at the bottom of the clock.

'Half past six?' I knew it was wrong before he shook his head. Mum came into the dining room from the kitchen. She had listened as the weary lesson droned on.

'Perhaps that's enough for today?' She attempted to free me from the torment shared inquisitor and victim.

'I don't know what's the matter with her!'

Dad gave up on me and threw the clock face down on the table. My nose ran and my eyes clouded over. It was painful to breathe. What was wrong with me? Why couldn't I do it? What was it that made it so difficult? I would watch other children not able to read, to struggle cutting clear lines with scissors, clumsily fashion clay pots, unable to copy the lines of a flower onto paper or colour within a given space. Some would be defeated by simply reciting a poem or remembering the lines of a song; so many things that held no fears for me, so why did this one thing become such a cause of sorrow? The more I tried to bury my ignorance of time the more importance it assumed at home. I grew to hate the sight of the cardboard clock.

Then one day I suddenly understood. It made sense. I could tell all the times without hesitation. It was an unexplained miracle that relegated the hateful clock to the cupboard. How it happened I had no idea. I still had to live with the legacy of 'taking so long to 'do it', but it released me from those sessions of fear.

My early memories included the fear of darkness. A terror that necessitated Mum keeping the landing light on until I had gone to sleep; I imagined hands reaching up from beneath the bed quietly pulling at the bedclothes. One day, in order to brighten up my bedroom, Mum and Dad obtained a Walt Disney Bambi poster and had stuck it on the wall. The delightful bright-eyed dappled fawn appeared to wink at me before it grew dark, but later, as I woke from a restless sleep, the pavement light shone on its unblinking eye. Its malevolent stare terrified me. By the next morning I cried to have the poster removed.

But most days I was a happy child copying songs from the wireless; singing my favourite 'Catch a Falling Star' sung by the crooner Perry Como, imitating the strange eerie electrical voice of Sparky the singing electric piano on Children's Favourites on the wireless and joining in with 'Nellie the Elephant', 'The Runaway train', Burl Ives with 'I Know an Old lady', becoming misty eyed with Danny Kay's 'Ugly

Duckling', amused by Max Bygraves' rendition of 'I'm a pink tooth brush, you're a blue toothbrush', and not having a clue where the 'Black Hills of Dakota' were although I regularly asked to be 'taken back' to them.

Our wireless was a temperamental machine that would often 'go out of tune', crackle alarmingly and emit strange whoops and whines as we tried to adjust the knobs and dials. But although it had a mind of its own I loved the wireless and the programmes that were broadcast each evening or at the weekends. I remember listening, with a tightened chest, as the strange Journey into Space invaded our dining room, and looking forward to the train-track music, 'daa da daa, da daa da daa da daa', before the honey-toned and dashing hero Paul Temple and his wife Steve came on to solve numerous dangerous crimes and investigate mysteries.

I would sit at the dining room table colouring, painting and drawing as the 'Workers Playtime' troupe entertained in the factory workers. I had a cardboard cut-out child wearing just a vest and knickers on which I could hang an assortment of clothes, using the little cardboard tabs at each shoulder. I dressed and undressed the cardboard doll as I listened to the programmes. The wireless entranced me. We had no television but I recognised all the performers' voices and imagined their looks. I knew that Dan Archer was a ruddy-faced and kindly looking old farmer on his farm Brookfield; was horrified when Grace was killed in a fire, and would be personally affronted at the deception when they brought in a new actor to play a well known character. During the programme we would cause some annoyance for my Dad, who was an avid 'Archers' fan, as Heather and I would get an unexplainable fit of the giggles which interrupted his concentration.

'Another pip out of you!' was a warning that simply had to be met with an almost inaudible 'pip' response from us which caused a new uncontrollable fit of giggles. Then we would be banished to the cold front room, having to wait until the programme was over.

By the time I started school Heather was having piano lessons at her junior school with the piano teacher Mr Mears. Having to play in the cold front room was not an attractive proposition and so Heather would leave her practise until it could no longer be postponed. The thudding keys would carry her resentment from the lounge into the warm kitchen. A mistake would be repeated with louder variation as she struggled to co-ordinate both cold hands whilst simultaneously reading the music score which had been graffitied with Mr Mears's corrections and pencilled instructions. A final crash of cords would signal the end of the practise and Mum and I would exchange a smile as the lid came thudding down. On some evenings Dad would fancy 'tinkling the ivories' and he would play a selection of pieces 'by ear', as he never learnt to read music, to entertain us.

Our education was important to Dad. One early evening a salesman came knocking at our front door. He was selling volumes of beautifully bound Encyclopaedia Britannica and dictionaries. Dad always found it difficult to say no and so we ended up with the complete set which was paid for over a very long period of time. If ever we asked a question or how a word was spelt we were referred back to the thick, heavy, unwieldy, reference books.

And since both Mum and Dad would not countenance any unauthorised absence from school Mum was horrified to find a Truancy officer at her door one afternoon demanding to know why Heather was not at school that day.

"If you come up the stairs with me you will find my sick daughter in bed!"

Mum was furious at the suggestion that Heather had 'played truant'.

"And I have always sent a letter back with her to explain if she has been ill!"

Mum could be a formidable figure when roused; a veritable mouse roaring at a lion.

On fine days we would plunder knobbly lumps of white chalk from the front garden and use them to draw our hop scotch squares on the outside pavement. Our skipping ropes, cut from a spare bit of washing line, provided hours of entertainment as we sang our way through endless ditties, but since the pavement outside our fence was rather narrow we had to cross over the road to the wider path if we wanted to join our ropes together for the more competitive games with our friends. I was still too young to go 'across the park' although I yearned to climb over the stone wall and investigate new horizons as I had seen other children do. We were allowed to go down the dirt lane and find delicate perfumed violets amongst the moss, and then later, cuckoo pints in the hedge row. Bringing them home to Mum she would find an egg cup to accommodate our treasures. The dirt lane led to the park gate and also to an old golden walled half-timbered house. The high hedge and gates deterred any impromptu visitors and noisy children. Although I could view most of the house from my bedroom window, despite watching for minutes on end, I never saw its occupants at the small windows or in the secluded gardens. I longed to know who lived there and what they looked like but my watchful efforts proved to be fruitless. Finally I adopted the house as my own since it did not have any obvious owner referring to it as 'mine' in my dreamy thoughts. Years later, when reading Thomas Hardy's 'Far from the Madding Crowd', it became Bathsheba's farm house in my imagination.

At the end of School Lane, on the corner leading to Willington Street there used to be a couple of heavily laden cherry trees just behind a garden wall. They tantalised us. Once, when we thought that no one was looking, we climbed onto the wall and stretched over to 'scrump' the fruit from the nearest branches. Suddenly the owner came rushing out into his garden. He must have spotted us from his window. We were lucky to escape without a mishap and we never dared to do it again.

One Christmas we were invited to a children's party at the grand Bishop's Palace in Maidstone. As Dad was working for Barcham Greens Ltd at the Hayle Paper Mill in Tovil the employees' children were provided with a Christmas treat. We had a tea, met Father Christmas and carried home two lovely boxes. Mine contained a set of nose, eye, glasses, and ears for a Mr Potato game.

It must have been sometime in the springtime that Mum took Heather and I to visit Hayle Mill in Tovil where Dad worked. Perhaps it had been an outing and we were waiting for Dad to finish work. I can't remember why we were there, but we found a door that led out onto the mill pond. A tranquil scene met our eye; tall bulrushes fringed one side of the lake, small darting iridescent blue damselflies skimmed across the water and in the distance we could see two magnificent swans. As we watched one lifted its wings into a perfect arc of snow-white feathers. We walked around the edge of the lake and then became aware of the sound of water splashing. One of the swans was half running, half flapping its wings, as it gathered speed, across the pond directly towards us; its long neck stretching out.

Mum held tightly onto my hand and suddenly we were running around the building. Frantically she pulled at locked doors trying to find which one had let us out. The swan was almost upon us; rising out of the water its wings now wide open it started to lunge itself at us. We were shrieking with fear as Mum tugged on another door handle. Back and forth we ran desperate to escape. Hissing and flapping the swan parted its beak and pecked at Mum's leg. An unlocked door finally gave way as we rushed through before clanging shut leaving the angry bird outside. We looked wide eyed at each other and then down at Mum's leg. The blood was dripping down her shin.

Afterwards we were told that the pair had a nest at the far side of the pond and probably the cob had seen us as a threat to his young brood.

We rarely had outings other than going to Gran's or down to the town to shop, but one weekend we were invited to go to Leigh-Pemberton's private estate with Dad's Maidstone Model Engineering Society. We were given a lift in Mr Wallis's magnificent roomy old car smelling of leather and wax polish. It regally wound itself through the roads and narrow lanes until we reached the huge house with its magnificence woodland grounds. A narrow gauge railway track snaked through the trees, passing through dark tunnels and over stone bridges. It was a child's fantasy. We climbed aboard sitting inside the little covered carriages and then off we went speeding round the bends, passing bushes and trees accompanied by hoots, whistles and puffs of smoke.

Heather went missing for while which started to worry Mum. Finally she arrived back at the little station.

"Where have you been?" demanded Mum angrily. You are not to go off on your own again!"

Later Heather owned up that she had walked through the long dark tunnel on her own just to see if she could. She had given herself a 'dare'.

"You could have been killed!" shrieked Mum, "What on earth will you do next? You naughty girl!"

She calmed down eventually and then we were able to eat our sandwiches and drink large mugs of tea that were being handed out to us visitors.

Once or twice Mum also took us to visit an Aunty who lived in a little terraced town house in Campbell Road just off Stone's Street. Petite, bird-like Aunty Addie was a Great Aunt to my Mum. Her sister had been my Grandma Kempshall's mother, Louise, whom we called Grandma Burley to prevent any confusion. Her house was crowded with Victorian furniture and interesting knick knacks. At her front window was a stand which held long rectangular crystal bars that caught the afternoon sun, cascading rainbows across the room. She was an excellent pianist and possessed a pretty upright piano which stood along one wall. In the small back parlour she had a huge gramophone with a brass coloured trumpet shaped horn and a stack of 'His Master's Voice' black 78 records. We were allowed to explore her little back garden. The gloomy house had been 'two up and two down' but had seen some expansion so the back parlour opened onto small kitchen before reaching the back garden. Dotted along her back path were some vivid red and mauve anemones and a line of bright yellow marigolds which I thought were so old-fashioned. She busied herself in the kitchen making us some toast for tea and proceeded to butter then sprinkle with sugar on the top which we had never tried before. She lived with her son Bob who seemed conspicuous by his absence as I never recall meeting him.

Since we rarely called on any of our relatives they remained as strangers throughout my life. Our visit to Gran's brother Donald was the same. He had the similar birdlike physique as Aunty Addie but with a long face and sharp nose. His wife Phyllis was quiet and nervous; she seemed almost frightened of her own shadow and her voice was so soft that we had to almost lean towards her to catch what she was saying; her slim nicotine-stained fingers held a long cigarette and the smoke swirled over her. Again their bungalow in Cranbourne Avenue just off Plains Avenue seemed dark and intimidating. Conversation was stilted and awkward as I sat fidgeting wondering why we had come and when we could leave without causing offence.

But the worst visit had to be going to see Aunty Elsie at her neat orderly house. She was a sister to Gran's husband but unlike gentle Will, Elsie exuded confidence; her sharp voice and no nonsense manner thoroughly frightened me. The conversation appeared to be more of an interrogation as she fired off questions that demanded answers. Years before, when Will had been in hospital, Gran had settled Mum to stay with his parents and taken young Betty to stay with Elsie whilst she stayed up in London to be near him. When Will recovered and was able to return home, Gran went to fetch Betty but Betty shrank away from her, hiding behind Elsie's skirts, not recognising her own mother after such a long absence.

"Do we have to see her again?" I whined when we finally set off home. "I don't like her!" But family duty had to be honoured for some reason.

Mum's younger sister Betty was altogether a different proposition. She knew exactly how to put us at ease and make us feel at home. Unfortunately she had not been able to have children so she indulged us. Her neat privately-owned dormer bungalow in Penenden Heath was light, airy and modern. Betty worked at the electrical company, Oswald Jones in town; she was their book keeper, wages clerk, secretary, receptionist, and general administrator all rolled into one, basically ensuring that the business ran smoothly and efficiently. Although she had very bad asthma attacks she didn't allow it to stop her leading a busy life, but there were times when her shortness of breath was quite alarming for those around her especially when she was eating as she had to gulp in some air before being able to chew her food, then snatching more air before the next mouthful.

Her skills as a needlewoman were evident in the embroidered tablecloths and tapestry cushions around the house. Being practical and efficient; she was able to mend a fuse, fix a leaking washer and attended to all the minor repairs and decoration in the house. The modern kitchen reflected the best 1950's design. In her uncluttered lounge, with its brightly polished parquet flooring, her leather G Plan three piece suite spoke of style and sophistication to my enamoured eye. We gleefully tucked into the tea which she had laid out in the small dining room, quite sad when we had to take our leave so that we could catch the bus back home.

If her husband Alan was there it became more difficult, as his 'larger than life' joviality and booming was quite unsettling. He was an imposing man with a love of aircraft and jazz, and he owned a car. He would attempt to recall all the details of model, airspeed, altitude and other technical information that left me nonplussed and then finally very bored. His hobby involved visits to airports, watching planes taking off and landing, whilst keeping a log of the day. Droning on and on he became more and more animated until Betty would announce that tea was ready and allow us some relief from the monologue. But after tea we would be coerced into sitting back in the lounge and listening to his jazz collection. Fats Waller and Jelly Roll Morton seemed to me to be more like names of sweets than people. The drum solos were especially mind-numbingly boring.

"Well what about that!" he would announce triumphantly after the piece finished. I didn't want anyone to make a polite comment as it would only encourage him to slip the next record from its sleeve, and prayed for Mum not to be nice, 'just for the sake of it'.

'Please don't!' I closed my eyes hoping that we could make our escape. But it was too late, another Boogie-woogie, Ragtime Band record slid on to the turntable, and we watched, dismayed, as he carefully lowered the stylus onto the groove.

Finally my infant days at School Lane came to an end. We had to take a series of tests before we left that summer. I knew that there were to be tests but my understanding of the significance was woefully inadequate. I also thought that tests, like races, had to be completed at breakneck speed. There was a test for the multiplication tables from the two times up to the twelve times oh so easy! I galloped through the lines. There finished. Well ahead of everyone else!

"And have you checked them Julia?" I stared at her, no need for that, I was well ahead; everyone else had barely got halfway through! I shook my head and handed the paper back. I can still see her look as she cast her eye down the sheet. I was appalled as I met her eye. Did I get some wrong? Was it all too late to change?

"So careless Julia," she sighed and my throat contacted as I saw her disappointment. It was too late I had refused her offer to check my work.

And then there was a test with sentences, pictures and little squares in which the choice had to be made with a little cross. I looked at the third sentence. Was milk yellow, or white? Tick in the box. What a strange choice. Milk was neither, yellow or white, what could I do? I wanted to write that it was a creamy white; the lightest of yellows according to the colours of my Reeves paint box. I mixed a hint of yellow with white when I painted a bottle of milk, so what was the solution. I finally made up my mind. Since there was no colour in white it would have to be a palest yellow therefore I would tick the box next to yellow. Again I handed in the sheets of paper and saw her glance at the responses.

She frowned. "Why have you marked this box?"

I hardly knew how to explain. "Well milk is creamy and there wasn't a box for creamy so as white has no yellow at all I had to put yellow because the cream at the top of the milk is more yellow than white..." my voice trailed away as she slowly shook her head.

"Oh dear," she murmured sadly.

I had no way of knowing at that time what my choices and insane need to race through work would lead to. It was years later that I realised that her sadness was only for me but for a system that penalised impetuous, carelessly clever and dreamy children; that her knowledge of my capabilities were secondary to the bland tests that they had been given to assess the children in their care.

For me I had the summer holiday in front of me and friends to share the days with. I had learnt new games; marbles were the latest attraction and I had a good hoard of them at home. Some were just the ordinary ones with a small swirl of colour through the centre but others were real pearls. They had smoky, translucence colours that appeared to change depending on how the light struck them. They were real large beauties. Their rarity and size made them far more desirable and therefore worth more in the game. I invited a friend to play. He had a sizable bag of marbles that I was anxious to acquire. I had no idea whether he was any good. But the greed of seizing his stash of marbles outweighed any valuation of the task ahead. I would just simply win. I had a good eye and a steady hand. What could stop me from winning the prize? It was only as my bag of marbles shrank with each turn that the realisation that I could possibly lose all came to me. My prized beauties had to be sacrificed in order to win back those that I had just lost. And then it was all, over. I had lost them all. I mourned the loss of those 'pearls' for many weeks and never played again. Mum saw my tears but I couldn't explain how the largest of my collection, the white smoky opal blue smooth beauty, simply couldn't be replaced. I had again been too sure of myself and had lost everything.

Going to the public library at the 'New shops' on Northumberland Road, gave me a great deal of satisfaction. The acquisition of a lending library ticket of my own made me feel so important. I whined and begged to go there regularly to exchange a book for another until I had managed to read all the Malcolm Saville books before starting on Arthur Ransome's Swallows and Amazons revelling in the detailed maps that accompanied each story. The trouble was being able to acquire them. So often the shelves were devoid of anything that I wanted. I had to make do with Enid Blyton, rather than CS Lewis's tales of Narnia, Billy Bunter stories or tales of girls in boarding schools chasing hooded robbers and strange apparitions in the middle of the night. First I joined Malcolm Saville's Lone Pine Club which gratifyingly provided me a newsletter and a card formalising my membership together with a shiny badge. Finally I grew tired of the limited choices available to me and hankered to borrow books from the adult section. That of course was out of the question. My ticket was valid for children's literature, nothing else.

My book reading was supplemented with copies of 'The Eagle' and then later the 'Girl' comics which were delivered weekly. Heather and I fought over who got their hands on the comic first. Inevitably as the oldest she won the fight so I had to wait impatiently itching to get my hands on it and catch up on the latest adventures of heroic Dan Dare facing his arch enemy, the lurid, queasy looking green Mekon bobbing on a saucer with his short little legs and huge head. I craved reading matter, desperate to find something that I could read whilst curled up in the small armchair in the dining room. At times the desperation to finish the story; to find out how it would all end, overcame my dedication to the text and I would skim the pages taking in the gist until finally the plot was unravelled. Dad took my fast reading to be a personal insult. Taking the book from me he would start to interrogate my ability to recall different parts of the story which were bewilderingly out of context. I would be baffled by his questions and confused by his direct gaze. I had drunk in the mood of the story and the emotion of the characters and suddenly had to account for sequences and events that had not seemed relevant at the time.

"You see, yet another book not read properly!" He would be annoyed by my casual disregard for time and detail. He approached each task with care and precision; a trait that Heather inherited. My 'it will do' and 'leaving things to the last moment' attitude exasperated him.

"I'm sure she enjoyed it didn't you?" Mum attempted, as she had to so many times, to smooth the tension out and clear the air but her intervention merely made matters worse.

"Well she'll never learn if she goes on like that!" He threw the book down on the table in disgust. I pretended to not care but his words cut through me. I knew that I should slow down and savour each word but try as I might the awful urge to know would rise up each time and I would gallop headlong towards the end. In so many things that I attempted I had to find the shortest way to complete the task, and my carelessness meant that erasers had their work cut out to correct mistakes.

"It's a good job that you are not writing with a pen," Dad would remark as I re- wrote my stories.

"When you start the junior school perhaps they will expect the work to be done in ink and then where will you be eh?"

But when it came to the garden and the wildlife contained within the flowers and bushes, time itself slowed down. I would watch enchanted as a ladybird spread her wings out from under her glossy red coat. I would be lost in wonder as a long, smooth, grey slow worm inched its way around a stone finding a safe place to rest or the articulated headed grasshopper carefully stroked and groomed its long antenna. Once we visited Maidstone Museum and went into the natural history section. I was delighted by the large boxed bee-hive situated by a window so that the bees could enter and leave their hive through a transparent pipe. They wiggled and fussed over each other in their busy-bee routine. The rest of the gloomy rooms held display cabinets of stuffed animals, birds, insects, butterflies, moths, and fish, with one set of drawers containing rows and rows of bird's eggs all accompanied by handwritten labels. The stuffed animals glared balefully back at us, their marble eyes catching the light.

If our adopted black cat decided to curl up on my lap I wanted to stroke his coat for ever but he was not a lap cat by nature and rarely decided to sit with me. Sometimes he could be induced to come upstairs at bedtime and enjoy the warmth with me on a cold winter's evening. I would try and hide him from Mum as I knew she did not allow it.

"Is that cat up there with you Julie?" His green eyes opened at the sound of her voice and he started to purr. I willed her to believe me.

"No," I tried to sound innocent.

"Well he went up those stairs I am sure of it."

I would hear her reluctantly climb the stairs to check on us both. I willed the cat to keep still, to lie undetected, but her entry into my bedroom meant that his detection was inevitable. She would haul the cat from underneath the bedclothes despite my pleas to let him stay.

33

On sunny days, during the holiday, we would beg for old sheets and blankets, and using the old clothes horse would attempt to construct a tent house in the back garden. Using copious amounts of string tied to the outside toilet door, we would manage to construct almost four walls and a sunken roof that threatened to droop further, as we struggled to put in a mat floor and cushions for chairs. Sometimes we pulled rose petals from blooms and sitting inside would mix them with water and sugar in little plastic cups and then present Mum with the 'perfume' concoction. We begged sugar to mix with water to make our 'tea' and then attempted to have a tea party before the walls and roof finally caved it on us. Time and time again we rebuilt our fragile house structure until exhausted by the effort we finally gave in and dismantled it. If it was really hot Mum would take down the galvanised tin bath hanging from a nail in the coal shed and fill it with tepid water so that we could have a 'paddle' in the back garden.

Not having many toys meant that those we had were precious to us. My favourite panda with a large yellow bow, went missing one day and was never found but my little toy terrier dog was brushed until it was almost bald and has survived until this day. Our Aunty Betty gave us her teddy bear with its bare muzzle and thin fur, and we shared an old trike until our cousin Tadek from Nottingham sat on it and broke it during one visit.

One afternoon we heard a plane flying low over the house. We rushed out to see what was happening. It was a biplane and as we wildly waved our arms to it, it waggled its wings before completing a circuit and flying off. Later we found out that it was our Polish Uncle Marian, Tadek's Dad, who had a pilot's licence and was able to fly short distances. It was something that we were able to boast about for some time.

Those hot summer days meant that we were always thirsty but I hated the taste of our chalky Kentish water. Poured from the tap into a glass it swirled sluggishly chalky white until finally settling and clearing. We waited for Tuesday to arrive and with it the box of groceries from Skinners. Mum would always order just one bottle of Tizer. We would greedily ask for a glass a soon as the box had been set down on the kitchen table.

"Well once it's gone it's gone until next week" we would be warned. But the taste was irresistible and we would gulp it down watching as the contents receded at an alarming rate. Sometimes we managed to make it last for two days but rarely longer than that.

When Dad worked for a short time at Edward Sharps & Sons toffee factory he brought home a bag of poorly wrapped toffees on a Friday night that each employee was allowed to take each week. Sweet rationing had finished by the time I was three but even after that we only had sweets for special occasions so the bag of toffees was a real treat for us. The bluebird wrappers were carefully folded back as if they still contained the toffee and we used them later in our imaginary sweet shop play. Dad would hand over his wage package to Mum minus his tobacco money and she would keep the rest. On the following Monday Mum and I used to walk up to the 'top shops' along Northumberland Avenue, queuing outside the Council Office to pay our £1 a week rent money.

Sometimes we were allowed to select our own sweets and I would choose the sweet red tipped cigarettes pretending to 'smoke' them in a nonchalant manner. Eventually I got fed up with smoking them and attempted to suck the end until it became razor sharp and pointed By the time I had 'smoked a few' of them my tongue was sore from the sharp sugar. Another of my favourites was the gob-stopper of which Mum thoroughly disapproved.

"One day you'll swallow it and choke yourself to death!" she warned.

But the ever changing colours of the gob-stopper had to be constantly admired. There was no way that the sweet could be hurried for one thing it was far too hard and it also was so large.

"Look at it now!"

"It's gone blue."

"Mine's pink. Look!"

Many a time, when enjoying a sherbet dip in the yellow bag I would suck the hollow black liquorice stick too vigorously and end up choking on the white fine powered sherbet.

There were special ways to eat each sweet or biscuit. A large wagon wheel had to be nibbled around and around, the square multi-coloured Liquorice Allsorts had to have its layers peeled off and eaten one at a time, a marshmallow needed to have all the chocolate removed from the top and then there were the ice-cream competitions. A wafer ice-cream could have the edges licked and then the wafer gently squeezed until the ice-cream started to protrude from the sides. This could then be carefully licked again until just a smidgen of ice cream was visible between the soggy wafers. Ice-cream cones were quite different. The ice-cream could be carefully licked to avoid it running down the sides but then it was gently pushed down the cone with your tongue. As the rim of the cone became devoid of ice-cream this could be nibbled back and the whole process begun again.

"Look I've got loads left."

"So have I."

"Yes but you started with more than me!"

The melting heat would make the game fairly difficult to execute, and it was touch and go who would still have some ice-cream left.

At Easter Heather and I used our eggs to set up a play shop on the round dining room table. Our Aunty Betty would always give us a lovely egg each with our names written on the dark chocolate in coloured icing sugar. They would command the best position in the shop with others grouped around them according to the style of the box. Terry's dark chocolate eggs were also a firm favourite, especially as in later years they were sold with a small selection of chocolates nestling under the egg in a beautifully designed box. Our temperamental cash till would not always flag up the correct amount in pounds, shillings and pence and sometimes when attempting to open the cash drawer to get the change it would spring out so suddenly that all the plastic money would shoot out. We spent most of the time artistically arranging the eggs and fighting with the cash till rather than 'selling' our produce to Mum .Eventually we couldn't resist the chocolate and our stock would dwindle. On one particularly warm day we didn't realise how vulnerable our eggs were and we came back to resume our play only to find our produce had begun to melt. After that we always made sure that the eggs were removed from their boxes before setting up our stall.

It was around that time that Dad completed a magnificent fairy tale castle for us complete with a moat, turreted towers and castellated walls. In the model shop in Stone Street, Maidstone, we could buy beautifully modelled knights; some on horseback holding removable lances and others welding axes and double edged swords. We took turns to 'hold' the castle against the invaders and many a horse floundered on their way across the drawbridge repelled by archers concealed on the ramparts. At times the drawbridge would be raised and a long siege would take place. Later Dad fashioned a miniature brass cannon that could fire used match sticks with deadly accuracy and fell the most intrepid soldier. Unfortunately the tiny lever used to load the spring before releasing the matchstick was extremely stiff and many a time real blood was shed during the battle as the lever sprang back and caught our fingers. The cannon was not only accurate but also if we didn't raise the barrel sufficiently the loaded matchstick would fly out with such force that it would gouge a small line in the dining room table. It wasn't until we had been playing for some time when Mum finally noticed the marks and threatened to ban us from playing 'once and for all'. Dad wore a sheepish expression that turned into a grin and a wink once she had disappeared back into the kitchen. We were more careful with the cannon after that, although a bit of spit, rubbed on the most recent gouge mark, was a tactic that we frequently employed to disguise our misdemeanours.

On sunny days we had the Golden Syrup tins that Dad had pierced and strung with thin rope for us to balance on to use as stilts. Holding on tightly to the two ropes we would clip-clop up and down the paths risking broken ankles as we became too confident in our newly acquired skills; trying to run before we could walk.

As summer came to an end we would see notices put up in the town announcing the arrival of the circus or a fun fair to be held in Mote Park. I recall little of the circus acts but the fairs left a vivid impression. The roundabouts and dodgems would be manned by sure footed,

37

swarthy young men as they balanced on the turntable flooring chatting up their young female clientele. Some moved lithely between the dodgem cars catching hold of the long poles as they advanced towards the cars, bending down to swing them dizzyingly around to the shrieks of delight from the young girls sitting inside them. The girls then tried half-heartedly to contain their full nylon netted skirts which threatened to billow out and show their bare legs and knickers.

Dad tried his hand at the coconut shy and despite maintaining that they were glued onto the poles he managed to knock one off its perch. We usually went home with a bag of limp goldfish and sticky cheeks and sore tongues from eating the bright pink candyfloss, which we had watched as it had spun around the revolving drum on a long stick in an ever-thickening silky web. And then there was a bag containing a coconut, which Dad had promised to crack open as soon as we got home.

In the autumn we knew that the best conkers were to be found under the horse chestnut tree by St John's Church in the park. We would arrive to find that a large group of children had got there before us and were attempting to bring down the prickly cases by throwing sticks up at the branches. As they cascaded at our feet we would all hungrily swoop upon them grabbing handfuls quickly, completely disregarding irate shouts of,

"Leave them they're ours!" from the stick wielding group.

Hauling home a bagful we would select the best ones for stringing up for a conker fight. As the fight became intense so we would end up with bruised knuckles due to our poor aim.

We also found chestnuts for roasting by the Keepers Cottage and Beech nuts under the huge sprawling tree just inside the park by the side gate; most of the time the Beech nuts were usually disappointingly unripe, or had begun to turn mouldy, rendering them inedible except to the squirrels who waited until we had gone to go back to their feast.

One cold snowy winter Dad decided to make a wooden sledge for us to use across Mote Park. We were both dressed in a pair his old trousers held up with thick twine to keep out the worst of the cold. We trudged off through crispy thick snow down the lane and through the little metal side gate towards the Pavilion temple where the best slopes were to be found. Already a crowd had gathered although the shrieks and whoops of delight greeted us before we saw them. We took turns to ride with Dad. One good push and we were off crunching and sliding over hidden lumps and bumps going ever faster as the snow flew up and stung our faces. Such exhilaration! As the afternoon sledging continued the slope began to glisten with ice formed by the paths taken by the sledges making each toboggan ride faster and faster. By the time the watery sun began to fade we were happily weary taking turns on the sledge being dragged home by Dad.

He also turned his hand to making a little stage lit by a set of electric footlights and fine wires strung across the top to allow for curtain and scenery changes. Heather and I made up little plays with cardboard characters bobbing across the stage. Next Dad made a tiny jointed fairy doll just for me. I'm not sure why he made her as I can't remember asking for one.

When Autumn arrived we enjoyed the glorious treat of joining Dad across the park with the Maidstone Model Engineers for their special evening 'fish and chips' run. We were allowed rides on the miniature trains lit by little lamps as we whizzed around under a starlit sky of black velvet, whilst my Godmother's husband, Sid Longley, made a wonderful batch of fish and chips for us, on his mobile fryer, which we ate from sheets of newspaper. The smell of chips wafting through the slightly smoky air was so inviting. We hungrily devoured our fishy portions with buttered bread rolls and hoped for more. Sid had a fish and chip shop up on the Tonbridge Road and had been a founder member of the society. He was a generous but gruff, shy man, but not used to children which made me quite nervous of him.

We rarely went on any trips but unusually one Saturday Mum had arranged for us to go to visit Woburn Abbey, although Dad was going to stay at home. Catching the bus we went into town and then got the train from Maidstone East before finally travelling on second train up to the Abbey. I don't remember anything about Woburn Abbey but only that when we finally arrived home late, very tired and weary Dad greeted us at the door. He had been waiting impatiently for us and quickly led us into the dining room where he had prepared a beautiful ham salad feast. There was an arranged the salad with sliced tomatoes and cucumber around the bowl, overlapping each other to create a whirl of colour. Sliced hard boiled eggs circled the ham. It all looked so pretty. I was amazed. I hadn't realised that food could look so wonderful and that he had the ability to be so self sufficient. I had never seen him prepare or cook anything in the kitchen so I suppose that's why the episode remained so vividly as a memory.

Dad had a 'thing' about Kent and castles so we also visited the fairy tale Scotney Castle as a family and the moat-surrounded Bodiam Castle, but our memorable trips were when we went down to Sissinghurst Castle where the author and gardener Vita Sackville West was still in residence. Our family lore stated that my Great grandfather had been head gardener there and had worked for Vita Sackville-West besides working on another large estate called Eastwell Manor. I was enchanted by Vita's 'secret' garden with its different areas of colour and fascinated by her tower where she wrote her books, but the herb garden with its pathway of herringboned bricks caught at my throat. I could not bear the smell of the curry plants, marjoram, aniseed, sage and thyme.

By the time that I had turned seven the nightmares began in earnest. Whereas I had only had an occasional bad dream that was quickly forgotten, now I could recall whole terrifying unrelated episodes that culminated in my waking, bathed in sweat, too fearful to allow sleep to catch me and plunge me back into the nightmare again. Fear made even breathing difficult and I would sob to be comforted. My father grew tired of the constant interruptions to their sleep and my fear was then compounded with the knowledge that he was angry with me. It was taboo to enter their bedroom even getting up out of bed without their permission was treading on very thin ice even if I had had the courage to do so. I resorted to knocking quietly on the wall where I judged that only Mum would hear me, praying that she would come to comfort me.

"Go back to sleep!" My Dad's exasperated voice quelled any further attempt to summon help. I would lie there exhausted wanting to sleep and yet afraid to do so. My sobs grew louder.

"Don't keep giving into her!"

"She's not going to settle now."

I listened to their muffled argument catching snatches of disagreement. Finally Mum would appear, sitting on the bed to rock me, patting my back as I tried to banish the scenes that had been so real.

"It's just a dream. There there. Just a dream."

But how could it have been so real and why did the same dream come back again and again to haunt my sleep? It would all start so beguilingly well until a slight feeling of apprehension that could not be ignored took hold. I had been playing with friends but they had been called away so I took to my wings and flew around the houses. Slowly I realised that I was losing height. I did not want to land in this place. It was not a place that was good. A bad place, with bad things in it. Then I would be running, desperate to get away from the things that threatened to tear me apart with their long thin arms and snatching fingers and I would be running and running along a narrow path hedged with tall green bushes. I would attempt to leap from the ground spreading out my arm-wings that I had been using so well at the beginning. But now the leap was not sufficient to gain enough height. I flapped my arms but they were useless. I could feel them getting closer and closer, the ground was thudding, my heart pounding they were upon me and I was lost.........!

And then awake; hardly able to catch my breath.

The house in the distance was surrounded by a meadow; a lovely house built on a low spot, its pretty garden planted with tall blue flowers and grasses. But really not a good spot to build a house as the river that ran through the meadow could break its banks. Was the river getting wider or was it just my imagination? I needed to be away from the meadow; but where to go? Where was safe? Go to the house. Inside the house the walls were running with water. The carpet on the floor was changing colour getting darker. Why was it darker? Was it wet? It was wet and the water was running down the stairs. I needed to get out of the house and on to high land. It was a trap. I needed to fly from the water that swirled around my feet. I tried to run in the wet grass. I could hear the roar of the water as it crashed over the fields towards the house. The river had changed course and it was coming for me. It knew that I had hidden in the house; it knew I was there. Run, run faster, jump up spread my arms, quickly, fly away......I am lost...........!

The shock of waking once again. Not able to breath. My head thumping with the roar of the defeated water; it would bide it's time until the next time I surrendered to sleep.

Everyone was downstairs in the kitchen. I was in the bedroom upstairs at Gran's house, her dark house. We had just had tea and they were washing up; clearing away the dishes in her green and cream cupboards. Why was I upstairs and not with them? Had I been sent upstairs out of the way? Who had sent me away? I could hear their voices but not what they were saying. How many of them were down there? Could I creep down and listen through the bars of the banisters without being seen? What would happen if they knew that I was listening? I would just go down a few steps and put my head over the banister rail. Yes Mum, Dad, Heather and Gran were all there.

"She must never know."

"We will never tell her."

I can hear what they are saying and they are talking about me! What must I not know? I can see them holding on to their chins. They are pulling at their chins and the skin is loose. They are pulling their faces off and there is another face in its place................!

The horror left me shaking, wide awake too scared even to call out. How could something that was so real be a dream? I dreaded the same nightmares returning. They would begin so beguilingly happy, until the strange sense of unease; that things were too good to be true began to pervade the sequences. Dark holes drew me in, hands pulling me to them, smothering me until the awful claustrophobia of fear threatened to stop my breath. Long dark corridors would compel me to rush through them to reach the light. Demons and devils, witches and old crones would call me to them, attempting to use their soft voices to disguise their evil intentions, wanting me to be as one with them; to melt into their existence. I could not protect myself from them; always they would find the most secure hiding paces and call 'we're coming for you' in lilting tones, whispering conspiratorially to themselves as they grew closer. Mum put it down to eating cheese late at night. A nice warm drink would do the trick. I drank the milk hoping to be ignored by my nightly terrors, but still begged for the light to be left on much to my father's disgust. I attempted to put off having to go to sleep, asking that I could have just five more minutes to finish my book, and then just five more, until Mum's patience was also worn thin.

"Go to sleep this instant!"

It was time that I grew up.

Top: Front view of Oxford Road in 1949 and the back garden.

Right: Mum's books including a well-thumbed Mrs Beeton's cookery guide:

From the top: My christening in 1950.Mr Cummings is holding me and on the right my Auntie Joan is holding her new baby Kevin. *Bottom:* Mum and her friend with Heather and me and Mum and Dad outside their new council house

Top: A photo of the Payne family abt.1951.
Below: Me with a neighbours' cat aged about three at home and an official school photo taken at School Lane Infant School

Below: School Lane class, Stephanie far left & me 3rd from left. Two photos of 49 Plains Avenue. Dad's brass cannon & 'Can you go' Lexicon set from Gran's house

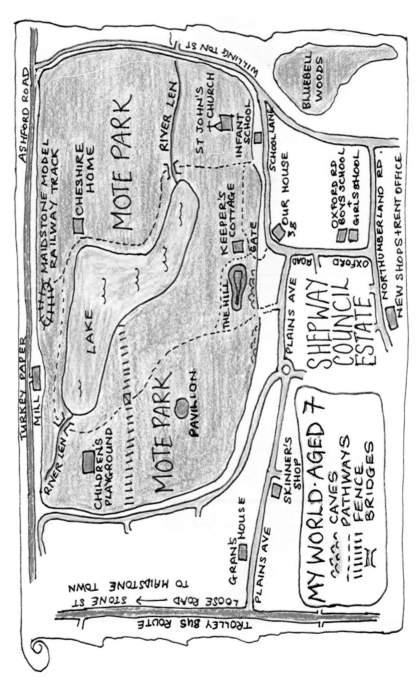

MY WORLD · AGED 7

᠊᠊᠊᠊ CAVES
PATHWAYS
||||||| FENCE
BRIDGES

MOTE PARK

ASHFORD ROAD

TURKEY PAPER
MILL

(THE) MAIDSTONE MODEL
RAILWAY TRACK

CHESHIRE HOME

RIVER LEN

LAKE

RIVER LEN

CHILDREN'S
PLAYGROUND

MOTE PARK

PAVILLON

GRANS
HOUSE

SKINNER'S
SHOP

PLAINS AVE

WILLINGTON ST

BLUEBELL
WOODS

ST JOHN'S
CHURCH

INFANT
SCHOOL

SCHOOL LANE

OUR HOUSE
38

KEEPER'S
COTTAGE

GATE

THE HILL

PLAINS AVE

OXFORD
ROAD

OXFORD RD
BOYS SCHOOL
+
GIRLS SCHOOL

NORTHUMBERLAND RD.

NEW SHOPS + RENT OFFICE

SHEPWAY
COUNCIL
ESTATE

TROLLEY BUS ROUTE

TO MAIDSTONE TOWN
STONE ST
LOOSE ROAD

PLAINS AVE

Chapter 2   1957 - 1960 New independence

I was reluctant to leave the infant school in School Lane as it had provided so much happiness and stability to my early years. It had given me a confidence in my abilities; but the move up to the Oxford Road Junior School for Girls was inevitable. Things were changing. In School Lane the Post Office had been pulled down, and a pub built in its place, called 'The Century'. On a late Friday night the drunks, worst for wear, would weave their way home, shouting abuse at imaginary slights, rambling to themselves and then singing snatches of tunes.

Heather had attended the first Oxford Road School which had been co-educational but as the numbers of children grew on the council estate the education authorities decided to accommodate just boys in the original building and put the girls in the new building right at the very end of Oxford Road with Miss Thorogood as the head teacher in charge. Although the school had large airy classrooms, a fine gym and spacious sports grounds I missed the company and cheerful camaraderie of the boys. My first teacher, Miss Hunt, was pretty and petite but although I was entranced by her, I was bored by her easy lessons.

Children were placed by the school in classes according to their ability. Due to my insane act of racing through the test papers in the infant school I was placed in the B stream. Subconsciously I decided to be the class clown and took to making my companions giggle, thereby interrupting the class lessons. Her solution was to move me around the classroom and to sit at a shared desk with a child that hopefully would not be lead astray. One day when my friend Stephanie and I continued to giggle uncontrollably we were sent outside with instructions to walk around the field and cool off. We chanted the multiplication tables, made cards for special occasions and inserted missing words in sentences and copied endless lines of letters. The days dragged on and so I became lazy. Time hung so heavy. When we were organised into small reading groups one afternoon I thought that I would have the chance to escape into my own world but instead of having the pleasure of 'silent' reading I was horrified to find that I was instructed to sit with those children who struggled with as they read out loud from simple, one lined sentence readers. My job was to correct their errors. It was a painfully dull job. I desperately wanted to explore the illustrated but unchallenging Beacon Readers adventure and fairy stories stacked together on the book shelves; to lose myself in the tales of bold William Tell and golden haired Rapunzel.

Children in the different classes did not mix together even when coming together on the yard at playtimes and so I viewed the children in Mrs White's 'D' stream with a mixture of curiosity and morbid fascination. One of her children wore leg callipers as testimony to the terrible crippling effects of polio. The girls in the 'A' stream looked down at us with a similar degree of distain. The atmosphere in the school thrived on a diet of petty squabbles and cattiness that little girls manage to perfect so well at that age. I became painfully aware of my appearance and the shabbiness of my clothes. I secretly coveted the pretty dresses and little white socks worn by my classmates and grew to hate my 'hand me down' skirts and grey socks that only stayed in place with a piece of tied thick elastic that left an indented red welt just below the knee. My lank hair could only be washed once a week and bath time was also a 'once a week' affair. Because nothing much was expected of me I didn't endeavour to achieve except when it came to art and craft or painting competitions. I relished submitting my pictures and was overjoyed to win paint brushes and water colour paint boxes as prizes.

At home I was given new responsibilities. When the coke and coal was delivered by the blackened coalman it was my job to check the pink order slip and count the bags that were emptied into the coal shed by the back door. Thankfully the correct amount was tipped in as

I knew that if there had been an error I could never have confronted the blackened-faced brusque coalman who would suddenly wink a white-lidded eye as he disappeared down the garden path. On Saturday mornings I either accompanied Mum to Maidstone to help her carry the bags of shopping home or stayed in to pay the various bills. There would be the milkman's money with the amount scribbled on an old piece of envelope or the premium book for the Pru man. I had to ensure that he took the brown ten-shilling note and returned the book properly annotated and signed.

I was fairly confident about these weekly duties but when the front door was knocked and I found a gypsy standing there with her bag of pegs and thrusting a sprig of heather towards me I could feel my courage fading.

"Lucky heather, buy my lucky heather dear." Her tanned, sun lined creased face was framed by a greasy black thick plait that was wound around her head like a rope. Her stained long fingers delved into her bag to produce long wooden pegs.

She edged closer to me, her stale foetid smell enveloping me.

"Bad luck will follow without it,"

The offer of heather was a demand rather than a request. I nervously mumbled that I didn't have any money and closed the door quickly hoping that she couldn't find her way to the unlocked back door. She muttered angrily as the door closed in front of her and I leant against the hallway wall my heart pounding uncomfortably. Then I crept into the front room to see if she had actually walked down the path or if she was still at the door.

"You shouldn't have opened the door." Mum was tired of repeating the same advice, and weary after her food shopping trip to town.

"Only open the door to the people you know."

One warm day when coming home from school I noticed that the council had started to paint the doors and windows of the houses opposite the school. As the workmen progressed in their work each day I realised that there was a pattern emerging. The first door was a mushroom colour; the next house had a blue door, then maroon and finally a green door. It was not apparent what colour we would have until the work commenced on our side of the road but I hoped for the pretty green or blue. Impatiently the work progressed sluggishly until they began on our 'even numbered' side of the street. I started counting; beige, blue, maroon, green, beige, blue, maroon, green until reaching our house. What a disappointment!

"We were going to be that horrible dark maroon." I indignantly informed Mum of the tragedy.

"Well it needs doing", she shrugged.

Not quite the response that I had imagined. Had she no taste!

"About time too," Dad learnt of the council's work, "and these blessed windows are shot through with rust again!"

He had attempted to eradicate the rust from when painting the windows inside but each time he carefully applied the Red Lead primer before the gloss white he would be infuriated to find that within a few months ominous brown stains of rust would begin to show through.

"Bloody rubbish metal," he would complain, "just cheap imported rubbish!"

Now that I was more able to help with household chores our visits to Gran on Saturday or Sunday became more frequent. Gran would decide on a job for me to do and despite my moans and groans I would have the task of cutting the front garden privet hedge with shears that could have done with a serious dose of sharpening. My manner of lopping stray branches replicated the Queen of Hearts designs on the unfortunate rose bushes. Chip, chop, chip chop, I impatiently trimmed the hedge. Then I had to collect all the stray bits and pieces of hedge that had fallen on the ground inside Gran's garden and outside on the pathway. My dignity was compromised by the curious stares of a couple queuing for the next bus at the bus stop right outside Gran's front gate. Gran would come down to 'see how I was getting on' which was a euphemism to see if I had missed any branches and if the work had been completed to her satisfaction. Inevitable there would be a Smiths crisp packet with its blue twist of paper for the salt or bit of newspaper that had been thrown over the fence by a waiting bus passenger which I had missed.

Creosoting the garden shed was another job that she also found for me to do. But once I had gleefully agreed to do it I was then dismayed to find out that the job also included taking out all the garden tools, dirty bags, and general shed paraphernalia that had been collected over the years before I could start on the task. Once again I had been thwarted. I hung my old coat over the branches in the pear tree as the surprising warmth of the spring afternoon made me hot and bothered. Once it was time to depart I pulled it off the branch and reluctantly struggled to put it on. Suddenly a painful stinging sensation made me tear the coat off and fling it to the ground. A large wasp was stuck to my arm. It had crawled up the sleeve of my coat whilst I was working.

I complained about the pain of my swollen arm all the way home as Mum and I walked back along Plains Avenue.

"Well, you should have left your coat inside the house!" Mum was fed up too and didn't have the energy to pacify me. I quietly seethed to myself about the unfairness of it all.

Another chore that I quite enjoyed was the task of mowing her lawn, albeit with a very ancient wooden mower that did not collect the grass cuttings. The only fly in the ointment for this work was my having to cut the path edges with the blunt shears and then to sweep the path clean according to Gran's eagle eye satisfaction. I enjoyed squirting oil on the rusty blades of the squeaky mower and liked creating patterned stripes ever widening and increasing around the fish pond.

When left to my own devices in the house and when Gran wasn't watching I would sneak her hats from the hall umbrella and coat stand and try them on in front of the mirror admiring myself whilst avoiding the hateful fox fur collar that she wore. Its tail fastened with a metal loop onto the chin of its marble-eyed face. I left that hanging forlornly on the hook. 'Poor thing,' I identified with its victim status. It was another reason to dislike my Gran. She didn't like me so why should I like her?

Our short visits to her at Christmas were a time of mixed emotions. There was the prospect of that special chicken dinner and presents in a pillow case although I knew by this time that I would not hear bells jingling on the rooftop or wake excitedly with the refrain, "Has he been?" Those lovely magical Christmases when I truly 'believed' were now just a memory. Only a couple of years ago I had been certain that I had heard the reindeers on the roof at home and on waking had felt the heavy pillowcase at the end of the bed.

"It's too early, go back to sleep" had been a warning from Mum and Dad until finally the first light of day allowed me to rush into Heather's bedroom so that we could share the delight of opening the pillowcase presents.

Accommodating us overnight meant that Mum and Dad had the large double bedroom at the back; Heather was allocated the small back bedroom, but I had to share Gran's lumpy feather bed. There was to be no argument; the matter had been decided. Christmas Eve arrived and I was put to bed in the cold room whilst last minute arrangements went on downstairs. Attempting to feign sleep I pulled the covers over my head as I heard Gran coming up the stairs and into the bedroom. Turning on the gas she lit the gas fire that popped and spluttered into life. I lowered the sheet to watch. First her stockings and dress were removed and hung over the bedrail. Next her long petticoat followed suit. She still had on her stays, vest and long baggy knee length knickers. Releasing herself from the confines of her boned stays she then removed her vest and taking a large tub of ointment from the dressing table and proceeded to extract a quantity of the liniment from the tub and rub it vigorously over her back and bottom. The smell of the ointment sickened me. I drew the sheet up to cover my nose and mouth; watching in fascination, not wanting to miss the performance.

Finally the lardy substance had been rubbed in sufficiently to her satisfaction and she put on her long nightie before removing all the hairgrips that had kept a grey sausage-roll hair piece in place around the nap of her neck. Not a word was spoken by either of us as she pulled back the covers and got into bed. The smell of the ointment followed her in.' It just isn't fair' I railed silently, 'why does it always have to be me!'

It may have been that night prior to Christmas or one like that when I awoke feeling sick. As I lay there I knew that I felt very ill. Struggling to sit up away from the feathered mattress I started to retch which in turn disturbed Gran from her sleep. Quickly she seized the chamber pot from beneath the bed and hauled me to the edge so that I was half in and half out of bed. As I vomited into the potty I wanted to come up for fresh air away from the sickening smell but she held me down fast by the back of my neck causing me to cough and sputter and then I attempted to wriggle away from her grasp as a terror of being suffocated took hold of me. I couldn't breath it was if I was drowning. Finally she relaxed her hold on me and I was able to catch my breath. It did nothing to endear me to her. Her roughness frightened me but somehow I couldn't explain how I felt to Mum when she came running into the bedroom just as the episode was drawing to a close. Afterwards when I played back the moment back in my mind; it was if I was being deliberately punished for being ill.

On Christmas Day we went downstairs for breakfast and afterwards received our presents in the back sitting room. The day did not have the same magic as it had at home. Mum always tried to let us down gently with the number of presents that we would have and that as usual money was very tight. My Godmother, old Mrs Longley, always remembered me. She would wrap up a box of pretty embroidered handkerchiefs or a selection of animal shaped soaps. Usually I got vests or other pieces of underwear from Mum and Dad. As I opened the parcels and tore off the wrapping paper my heart soared. Nestling inside was a cherry red corduroy pinafore dress and a sky blue jumper. I was so surprised and so pleased that the new dress fitted. No need to hem it up after Heather had worn the garment; it was new just for me. I was in seventh heaven that Christmas.

Christmas dinner was cooked by Gran. We were going to have a chicken! I had glimpsed the wonderful bird sitting in the roasting tin, and all morning was tantalised by the smell wafting from the cramped kitchen. Finally the plated meal was put on the table that had been set for us in the front room. I looked down at my plate. A single slice of chicken accompanied by the sprouts and other vegetables barely covered my plate. Glancing around I saw that a similar meagre amount had been allotted to each of us. I knew that the chicken had been small but had hoped for more. In no time our plates were empty. Mum looked across at me.

"Did you want some more?"

Before I could answer, Gran broke in, "we need to save some for tomorrow Joyce".

Nothing more was said. When we left to return home after the short holiday I remember seeing the chicken carcass on the marble slab in the kitchen larder. It had not been touched since Christmas Day and being unrefrigerated was probably unfit to eat by then.

'When I grow up I'm not going to save anything until tomorrow!' I thought angrily to myself. 'She is so mean that she would rather let it go bad than give it to us'. As usual I was quick to condemn probably drawing all the wrong conclusions. She had probably bought all the food in for us without having much of a contribution from Mum and Dad. Rationing in the war had taught that generation everything there was to learn about 'making do and mending'. At home we always had the most meagre of rations too. Sunday roast for the four of us comprised of a single thin scraggy breast of lamb; more bones than meat, never expensive beef or the 'only for high days and holidays' chicken. Mum would usually make us greasy fried spam fritters, mutton stews with dumplings, shepherds pie, stewing steak and kidney pie or suet pudding all of which had more vegetables, crust, pie or dumpling than meat.

"We'll have to send out a search party" was one of Dad's favourite sayings as we dissected the pie to find the meat.

Mum's prowess for making good dumplings and the lightest of flaky pastry was routinely praised by Dad. Sadly, although he knew that his wages were insufficient for a family of four, he still sent a ten shilling note a week up to his mother in Nottingham, taken from his £10 wage packet received from his employers at Hayle Paper Mill, until the news came in 1956 that she was seriously ill, being in the last stages of cancer. We travelled up by train to see her just before she died. She, and Father Payne, as we called our Dad's father, lived in Jacksdale in their small darkly lit house. In the gloomy bedroom I was aghast to see her lying in a little bed. Her skeletal frame hardly making an impression on the covers laid over her. She was a tiny sparrow, barely able to make herself heard; on one thin wrist hung her watch, now far too large for her.

She saw me looking at it. "When I die you can have it," she smiled.

I was horrified. I had not meant to stare and certainly had not been coveting her belongings. Mortified I looked away and took in the contents of the cold and desolate room. Her bedside table was a simple rough orange packing case. On the small mantelpiece above the unlit fireplace were two figurines; a swain and his lass in period costume each with their arm around the neck of a swan. I saw Heather looking at them as Chrissie, Dad's mother, followed her eye. "Oh yes, if you like them that will be something for you too," she murmured.

Heather and I looked at each other wide eyed not knowing what to say.

"Thank you," she managed to answer.

Afterwards we huddled together waiting for the grownups to take their leave.

"Did you see how thin she was?" she whispered. I nodded, shocked at all that we had witnessed.

We knew that we were poor but the shabby unkempt surroundings still made an impression on us and we were unaware of how much we were subsidising Father Payne's miserly habits.

"Tight old bugger," Dad was furious as we came away from the house. "Some things never change".

Mum's lips were pressed tightly together. Her thin mustard yellow coat had seen a number of cold winters and her shoes needed a decent sole if they were going to last much longer. Dad had already stuck on thin rubber ones with a nasty smelling thick treacle-like glue as he had done with his own polished shoes. Harold Macmillan might have told the country that 'we had never had it so good' but there didn't seem much of 'it' coming our way.

By the time I was in the junior school we two girls received our weekly pocket money of two shillings and sixpence. Dad had changed employment by this time and was working as the assistant engineer at

T&J Hollingbourne Ltd, Turkey Paper Mill earning £52.10 shillings a month. My half-crown was put into a little red Royal Mail letter box tin. I would routinely count it to see how much my savings had grown. We used our savings to buy birthday and Christmas presents for Mum and Dad. The tin box was supposed to be tamper proof so that money could not be extracted but I had found a way of inserting one of our bone-handled table knives into the letter box slit and tipping the tin upside down until some of the coins were retained on the ledge of the knife. With some gentle shaking the coins would then slide off the knife into my lap.

Heather and I had been consigned the small two cupboards on the dining room sideboard. Each cupboard came with its own little key. Within weeks my key had been lost with the contents of my side stacked and jumbled carelessly inside. My small treasures, money box tin, bag of marbles, books, paint boxes and toys were just about contained in the little space. Heather's side was a different proposition altogether. Her locked cupboard remained neat and tidy and often untouched, so my Christmas manicure set was too handy and was frequently 'borrowed' whilst her identical set never saw the light of day.

It was the same upstairs. My small bedroom with its piece of lino and bedside rug had an old chipped marble topped wash stand and a short built in wardrobe that was situated over the stairs. My meagre supply of clothes was kept in the drawers underneath the wash stand which was eventually replaced by a newer scratched second-hand dressing table missing its mirror. Heather's double sized bedroom had a built in wardrobe with hanging space, a dark wooden chest of drawers, a second-hand dressing table and a three quarter sized bed. In Mum and Dad's bedroom they had two built in wardrobes and a chest of drawers and dressing table that were both pieces of 'utility furniture'. There was a small fireplace in the room but it was never lit. No rooms had any heating and so Mum would have to carry up a smelly cylindrical paraffin heater when it got too cold which cast beautiful swirling patterns on the bedroom ceiling. We were given rubber hot water bottles to help ward off the worst of the cold. Once I fell into such a deep sleep before the heat of the bottle dissipated that I woke up in the next morning with a red blister welt on my leg.

Downstairs the house reflected our circumstances. The front room had a shiny black bitumen type of floor with a small rug in front of the fire. In the dining room there was a larger carpet square that seemed threadbare even when we were much younger. We looked shabby but it didn't start to bother me until I went to the junior school when my infant reverie seemed to clear. I started to make comparisons, being at first dismayed by them, and then ashamed of our circumstances. By the late 1950's some neighbours possessed a small black and white television set and my friends spoke of the programmes that they had seen; Andy Pandy, Rag, Tag and Bobtail, The Flower Pot Men with little Weed, Muffin the Mule and Sooty and Sweep. I longed to watch them too, not wanting to be an outsider. Some had also acquired a two-wheeler bike; our battered old tricycle had long gone by then. Years later I was given a pair of red leather strapped Jaco roller skates complete with a special spanner to make the necessary adjustments for sizing which became my pride and joy. But I am going ahead of myself.

Heather and I were as different as chalk and cheese. She was happy in her own company; I grew increasingly restless and wanted to be outside playing with other children. We argued and bickered over silly things which drove Mum up the wall.

"Why can't you play nicely like Mrs Lawrence's girls?"

We resented the comparison making rude faces behind her back, "goody, goody two shoes" we whispered conspiratorially. "Namby, pamby, too good to be true girls", we dismissed their allegedly saintly behaviour, at a loss at how to change our own ways. Sticking our heads out from Heather's bedroom window we could sometimes spy on them, playing so nicely, with their dainty dolls and tea sets sitting on a rug in the back garden.

Mum in turn grew frustrated at Heather's 'stubborn' ways. As she dug her heels in Mum's exasperation reached breaking point. After one heated exchange and clash of wills, Mum smacked her bottom with her hair brush; they both shrieked at each other, Heather at the pain and indignity; Mum realising that she could not be quell her rebellious daughter. I grew alarmed at the escalation of hostilities, frightened at what was to happen, until finally reaching breaking point; begging them to stop. "Please don't, please!"

They both drew back somewhat startled by my tears.

"Now look what you have done", shouted Mum as Heather escaped her clutches and flounced from the room.

That night, as many after that, Heather sought my alliance in her plan to run away.

"We'll go tonight when they are asleep."

I willing agreed whilst the daylight made me bold but once the black night descended so my courage faded. Heather would retreat moodily back to her room as I pathetically whispered an agreement to, "let's go tomorrow."

She knew in her heart of hearts that I wasn't up to midnight escapes.

As the first year at the Juniors wore on I became less and less enchanted with school. The neat writing lessons meant that we were given pens with interchangeable thin gold nibs and red and blue lined paper so that we could start to perfect a Marion Richardson writing style. Lines of looped and curved $hhhhhhh$ were joined with

$nnnnnn's$ patterns of letters repeated across pages frequently marred with blobs of ink as the nib decided to drip off the surplus ink when refilled from the desk inkwell and my uncertain fingers became purple dyed. Despite Miss Hunt's entreaties, "remember that the pen should not come off the page until the end of the line". The cheap scratchy pen nib refused to flow requiring constant refilling and blotting the page.

My first year report arrived in July 1958. The B grades reflected my lack of ambition and achievement. Miss Hunt's remarks for Reading stated that I was 'a good fluent reader. Understanding is of a high standard;' in Composition that I wrote with 'dignity and charm.' For Art and Craft which was not graded I had 'excellent ability; an imaginative use of colour and space'. In the General Remark section I apparently worked with 'interest and precision' and 'contributed to class work' had a 'good standard' of general knowledge and was 'critical and perceptive' in my work; although the cryptic last sentence stated that I was an 'interesting member of our class'.

When the local newspaper showed a picture of Miss Hunt's wedding in August of that year I was amazed. I had not realised that teachers had a life away from school. Her marriage to a Mr Winche who lived just a stone's throw away from my Gran in Plains Avenue astounded me. They had been conducting a romance without my knowledge. I cut the picture from the local gazette tucking it away with my other treasures.

The summer holidays allowed us to embark on outdoor adventures and later a visit to our Aunty Sally, Dad's sister in Nottingham. I was now allowed play in Mote Park although Mum would have disapproved of our method of reaching the park by scaling the high five foot stone wall that surrounded it. We were supposed to walk down the lane and go through the little side gate but finding small footholds in the rims and gaps spaced between the stone work was much more adventurous. We knew that swinging on ropes suspended from the trees could cause us to break a limb but we were fearless. Accidents happened to other children not us; we ignored the warnings. Stephanie and I loved to make dens in between the roots of large chestnut trees on the 'Hill'. We had permission to play until dinner time, although as we didn't possess a watch between us 'dinner time' was pure guess work. We would drop down from the wall on the park side and make our way through the Beech and Sweet Chestnut trees; skirt around the path leading to the small timbered house that had once been a park keeper's cottage and start to ascend the 'Hill' using the sheep trails and avoiding the stinging nettles and spotted dock leaves that the sheep didn't seem to like although they kept the rest of the grass trim.

Over to the left of the hill the park wall was very high, being well over thirty feet as the ground inside the park was much lower at that point. The deep, frightening, caves had not been fenced off in those early years but we still didn't dare go inside as we didn't have a torch to light the way. They were too dark and forbidding. Still we had no problems in climbing up the jutting rocks and finding little ledges to perch on, as we encouraged those below us to find footholds and handholds in between the rocks, so that they could join us on our high vantage point. Sometimes in our dens on the hill we would find evidence of other occupants who had attempted to light a 'camp fire' during their play. We resented their intrusion, finding the spent matches that were scattered around our den. Once some boys left a frayed rope with a piece of wood knotted on the end, tied on a branch above the den; we gingerly tested it with our weight, pulling it down as hard as we could to see if it would break free and then swung back and forth in a Tarzan style, each swing getting higher, with the aid of a extra good push, as our confidence grew.

I suppose it was hunger that drove us back home; our legs and skirts covered with dirt and grass stains. Sometimes we were later than expected, but more usually than not, our Mums appeared not to worry about our long absence. All the estate children in our road seemed to play in the park, it was assumed that someone would have noticed if something had gone awry and reported it back. We felt safe and secure, nothing could go wrong.

It happened one afternoon.

Dad had fashioned a strong wooden staff for Heather and I to use in our play. It was a precursor to our game of bows and arrows that we would later play together with him. We had scaled the wall as usual and were striding off to the hill and then planned to go down to the lake. As we tramped towards the 'park keepers cottage' we saw the two S--------- boys open the squeaky side gate and move towards us. My heart contacted. They were bad news. Perhaps they were just going to walk past us I prayed. The older one looked up towards us and I could see that he had focused on the staff that Heather held. They moved closer.

"Give us that stick", the older one sneered.

I attempted to fold myself behind Heather; my throat pounding with my heart beat. She didn't respond.

62

He moved closer and attempted to grasp the staff from her hand. She swung it away from him.

"Give it to us" he demanded again.

My head was pounding; fear froze me. I prayed for her to relent. 'Just give it to them so they go away'. I silently pleaded. But she was always so stubborn. Nothing would persuade her to give in.

"No."

Then I saw the penknife glinting in his fist.

"I'll stick this in yer if you don't do it", he threatened.

I caught hold of her skirt. 'We're going to die,' I thought.

They came closer to her. There was no escape. Suddenly he plunged the knife into the back of her hand. I started to wail and scream. She still held onto the staff and they backed away. Blood tricked round her wrist. They both saw the blood and began to back away. My screams and her resolute stance had unnerved them. Heather tired a grubby handkerchief around her hand. The blood quickly seeped through. We went through the gate following our assailants who had fled and were out of sight.

Mum washed and dressed the wound; her mouth was thin and pinched.

"Those boys will go from bad to worst" she drew in her breath sharply, "just wait until I see their mother."

Seeing that I had calmed down, she set off up the road to 'have it out' with Mrs S----------.

We were told that they would 'get what for' when their Dad came home and would not be allowed out for a week, but the very next day we saw them on their bikes riding up the road. They continued to be a menacing presence on the estate so we made sure not to be around when they were about if we could help it. I fervently hoped that they would indeed come to a 'sticky end'.

As well as the hill we had other play areas in the park which were a little further afield. Sometimes Stephanie and I would make the trek down to the tadpole filled stream towards the Willington Street entrance to the park, and then follow it back towards the stone bridge over the River Len, where we could throw 'Poo' sticks and watch them glide past. If we still had more time we would continue on the path and skirt around the large lake disturbing the yellow beaked moorhens who used the bulrushes for nesting sites. There were always a few swans to be found on the lake by Mote House and some hungry mallard ducks looking for bread crusts. At that time the park was grazed by both sheep and cows. Sheep droppings and cow pats were spread abundantly around the parkland. We followed the sheep trails around the water's edge watching as the cows munched, using their rough tongues to curl and grasp clumps of the grass. Sometimes they would lift their huge heads watching our progress and stamp a foot or shiver as the flies irritated them and then swish the flies away with switch of a tail. I kept a respectable distance from them. They were big beasts close up. I had heard that they could charge and trample people if threatened. I didn't want to be involved in a stampede.

On 'our side' of the lake there was a small island that we could just about reach if we carefully negotiated some precariously floating logs. We used them as stepping stones placing our feet in the centre of the log in case we sent it spinning round. Stephanie had previously gone along with her brother Stewart and some of his mates and had misjudged her step. She went crashing down between the logs. As she went under the water the logs closed above her head. Luckily Stewart was able to haul her out but then seeing her bedraggled hair and dress realised that they would be in a lot of trouble going home with her in that state. She had to wait until her dress dried and had to stick her head under a gushing water pipe to try and get rid of the weed and slime in her hair before they dared take her back home.

One afternoon a group of us took the long walk across to the fence that portioned the uncultivated area of parkland from the part that contained a children's play ground. In the play park was a grey metal witches' hat that swung dangerously to and fro from a central pole if older boys decided to stop the natural rotation, three or four swings; a long swing boat that had two long pulling ropes suspended from the top section, a wooden slatted roundabout and a high metal slide; all the pieces being set in areas of unyielding concrete. When we got there most of the equipment was in full use. We had to calculate

64

which child would relinquish their turn first, moving in when they felt too intimidated to continue their play. The trick was to rush at the vacated piece before another child beat you to it. Taking turns was all well and good when adults were around but a timid child would have stood all afternoon if they adopted that philosophy. We had no qualms in grabbing the ropes of the swing.

"Finished? "

We stated a claim rather than posing a question as the reluctant child was displaced, unable to continue, once one rope had been held fast. We took delight in making the swing fly higher and higher our legs pulling back and thrust forward to create wide arcs; the air rushing through our hair. Such exhilaration!

I didn't use the 'boat' if other older child took the opposite seat. Having only the rope to hold on as it rocked back and forth through the air meant that if it picked up speed you ended up being unseated and then banging back down on the seat as if you were on a very high seesaw. Once as I stood by the slide waiting to climb up the steps I watched as a small boy walked towards the boat. Being so small he was unaware that the boat was rushing down on its descent towards him. With horror I saw the tip of the boat strike him with full force on his forehead and partly lift him off his feet as it struck. He landed with a dull thump; blood gushing from the red-meat gaping wound on his head. At first there was no sound. It was as if anything had stopped. The suddenly the screaming began. Some adults rushed over, their shouts and his screams created a terrifying cacophony of noise and panic. His face became a mask of scarlet; meat on a butchers slab. I didn't dare look again; it had been too horrifying. We didn't stay to find out what happened next.

So the park became our constant companion. There were always new adventures and games to play. If we had become bored with making dens on our hill we walked further on towards the Plains Avenue entrance and down towards the lake to play on the 'ship'. This game centred around a vast fallen tree trunk that was surrounded by stinging nettles. The nettles had not deterred us children from swarming on it trying to occupy the best vantage point. Our bottoms had burnished the surface to a smooth and shiny copper shade. We became pirates ordering each other to 'walk the plank', which effectively meant that the victim had to leap off the side of the tree trunk whilst endeavouring to miss the numerous clumps of stinging nettles in the shark infested 'water'.

Each season brought its own delights. Walking down the lane to the park I loved to peer into the hedgerow to find celandines, violets, wood sorrel, and primroses in the spring. Later I gathered daises for daisy chains and picked buttercups.

"Let's see if you like butter." The golden glow reflected under our chins.

I marvelled in the strange and secret cuckoo pints; enclosing their upright brown centre within creamy green lips. As the days grew warmer my attention was taken by the butterflies, ladybirds and elusive green grasshoppers who seemed to keep up their constant rasping throughout the summer but fell suddenly silent if you attempted to seek them out.

"Ladybird, ladybird
Fly away home
Your house is on fire
And your children are gone"

We snatched up the long grass and held it taut between our thumbs before blowing through the clumsily arranged 'reed'. Raucous shrill notes would follow our progress as we searched for better 'instruments', competing to make the loudest call. Eventually our lips became so numb and our cheeks tight with fatigue that we had to stop. If we were thirsty we would pull out long stems of grass from their outer bindings and then suck the clean juicy stems. On the park wall, clinging with the tenacity that only bindweed had, we would grasp the bulbous stem of the white trumpet flower, "grandmother, grandmother, jump out of bed", and squeezing the end would watch with satisfaction as the white night gowned granny flew through the air.

At the end of Willington Street we were allowed to go to Bluebell Woods. There we could either take the 'high road' or the 'low road' as we named the two tracks.
"You'll tek the high road
and I'll tek the low road,
and I'll be in Scotland before ye."
We delivered the snatch of song with an awful attempt at a Scottish accent.
The woods were a blaze of blue in the spring. We were told that there were rare spotted orchids that we were not allowed to pick but I never found one. Most children on the estate gathered armfuls bluebells, taking the wilting blooms home the stems dripping with slime. But the woods never held the same fascination for us as the park did despite the tall Red Campions and white carpets of wood sorrel and wild garlic. The dense spread of thin trees on either side made any deviation from the path too difficult, and besides, the trees were far too spindly to climb.
Once, when we had gone for a walk in the woods with Mum, we met a man coming towards us. His coat flapped open. I saw a flash of bulbous pink sprouting from the top of his trousers. Mum bundled us briskly past him as we stepped up our pace.
"Come on Julie, Heather keep up!" She didn't usually sound quite so sharp on a walk. Eventually we slowed down; other walkers passed by and we nodded greetings.
"Silly man," she smiled reassuringly at me. "He could have caught his death, a cold day like today." The incident was already over, no need to worry.
On walking up our garden path, some antirrhinums had self-seeded. We softly pinched the 'bunny mouths' to open and close their mouths to make them speak.
 My most ignominious day involved the time that Heather and I joined some children in their play on the grassy slopes situated by the dividing fence line to the left of the large lake. The improvised game involved who could win the race down the slope. We panted back up the slope and rushed down again with endless energy until the last

disastrous descent when I lost my footing. I rolled down the slope faster and faster until I came to a stop almost unable to catch my breath. As I sat up my awful state presented itself to me. The smell was terrible. On my unchecked fall I had rolled in numerous cowpats. I was covered from head to foot in the foul smelling, dripping, cow muck. Merciless laughter and hoots of derision from the other children followed me as Heather and I started my tearful homeward journey. She grasped the back of my dress collar holding me away from her, propelling me unwillingly forward. I think she realised that I was frightened at what Mum would say and the reception that we would get. Through the park we trudged, with me trying to twist away from Heather's restraining grip on my collar and her trying not to let the cow muck get on her as I writhed and squirmed.

 Finally we trudged up the little lane, across the road and round to the back of our house. I can't remember what Mum had first said, but my dress and socks were removed, the tin bath which was kept hanging up in the coal shed was filled with water and I was scrubbed down outside. I think that Heather was blamed for not keeping a proper eye on me or keeping me out of mischief. That put another nail in our fragile sisterly relationship. She was furious that I had escaped the blame.

"I'm not taking you to the park again!" She flared at me when we were at last alone.

"Don't care, don't want to!" I retorted sullenly. My shame and humiliation was quite complete.

The summer holidays did not allow for unlimited play. Sometimes we were summoned to assist in household chores. Monday was still the designated day for washing. When we had first moved into 38, Mum had a kitchen boiler where all the washing would take place with little bags of 'blue', but later she acquired a very basic washing machine with a detachable rubber wringer. The whole area of the kitchen was commissioned. The small kitchen preparation table was moved into the dining room and the washing machine was hauled out into the centre of the room. First we had to fill the tub by connecting the long rubber hose to the hot tap on the sink before the soap flakes were added. A mangle mechanism, which had been folded down into the machine for storage, was pulled up and screwed back into place. Washing was pushed in; the lid closed and the machine started to wash and tumble the clothes. After a period of time deemed appropriate by Mum she dipped the wooden tongs into the scummy depths to pull out the 'whites'. Next a heavy steaming sheet would rise out and be fed into the rubber mangle. My job was to turn the side handle so that the excess water could be squeezed back into the machine. Each washed item would be put into the tin bath on the floor to await the rinsing stage. At times the heavy sheets became too bulky for the mangle to handle and became jammed so I had to reverse the process and Mum would hold on to the sheet and attempt to pull it straight before feeding it back in between the rollers. The water would be used again for the next load of clothes until the grey water became too cold to use. Our electric copper kettle and filled saucepans on the cooker would be boiled and heated to provide some extra heat for the final load. Eventually the whole kitchen would take on the clinging soapy damp smell of wash day.

The final stage was to empty the machine of the dirty water so that fresh water could be put in for the rinsing process. Once again the rubber pipe would be utilised, only this time being inserted into the side of the machine. Mum would press a button and the machine would start to empty. My job was to ensure that the water went down the sink and not on the floor. I had been distracted at one time and unwittingly let the pipe go, only for it to slither up and spray the kitchen with dirty soap-sudded water. Mum had not been best pleased. Once full of fresh water the process of rinsing and turning the mangle handle would commence. It seemed to take hours for the process to finish. Many a rubber button from a liberty bodice would be ripped off by the unforgiving mangle rollers, and then we had to hang the heavy washing up on the line that stretched up alongside the back garden path.

My job this time was to untie the white waxed rope washing line from it's figure of eight fastening and let the line down so that Mum could reach to peg up the sheets. As the weight of each item of washing dragged heavily on the line I had to be sure to hold on tightly to the end of the line, pulling it up a little each time to counteract the drag. It got heavier and heavier as the washing filled the line. Eventually it needed us both to pull on the line and fasten the end securely back on tot the post fittings. Even strong washing lines give way eventually. It was a calamity when it happened as all the wet washing ended up dragging through the mud in the vegetable plot. Mum had to redo all the washing with no chance of it drying in time. We had the smell of damp sheets hanging over the clothes horse for days until the new line was purchased and put up by Dad.

On especially hot days the kitchen became uncomfortable for Mum to cook in. Milk would turn sour and butter rancid as we had no refrigerator to keep them fresh. We fretted to have something cool to drink.

"There's water in the tap!" Mum would snap knowing that she couldn't afford to give us anything else.

"Don't want that", I would reply stubbornly. Our chalky water was horrible. You had to be dying of thirst before drinking it.

"Well you can't be that thirsty!" Harassed by us she would be sharper than normal.

"Oh, kids, cats and goldfish!" she would often exclaim. We had one stray black cat, Nigger, politically incorrectly named by Dad, who had eventually wormed his way in to the household and now took his meals on a saucer placed under the kitchen table. I had won some goldfish when visiting a fair ground held in the park, and of course the 'kids' referred to us. Later I acquired a white mouse called Monty. He lived in a little cage in the hall and I used to make him houses from a set of Lego bricks so that he could run around inside and peep out from the windows, his pink eyes round, his whiskers quivering and twitching, leaving little black seeded 'calling cards' in each room. When he finally died he was buried with due solemnity at the top of the garden, next to the rhubarb, in a little cardboard box. His grave marked with a wooden cross made from two ice -lolly pop sticks tied together with string.

Usually Mum took my bad behaviour and whining in her placid stride but one day I must have caught her at a difficult moment and had gone too far. Taking up the boiler stick she chased me around the kitchen table. After a couple of turns around the table, only just remaining out of reach, I took the opportunity and fled up the stairs leaping up two at a time; rushing into my bedroom and fearfully pressing myself against the door in case she attempted to gain entry. Putting my ear against the door, my ears thudding with my heart beat, I tried to hear if she had followed me but couldn't hear a sound. To be on the safe side I stayed inside and didn't attempt to go down to apologise until the end of the afternoon. During the next few days I made sure that she didn't find any occasion to be annoyed with me, not wanting to incur her wrath and a repeat performance with the boiler stick.

Splitting bad headaches regularly caused me to go to bed. I still suffered from constipation although Mum poured doses of Syrup of Figs and Liquid Paraffin down my throat. The thudding headaches would make me nauseous with pain. The only relief to be found was if I managed to sleep them off. It would seem to take for ever as I waited for sleep to release me from the pain.

We were rarely ill enough to take any time off school. Both Mum and Dad believed that if you were well enough to want to come downstairs then you were fit enough to be at school. Being ill meant that you were confined to bed. In the winter the luxury of a hot water bottle would keep us company. A wooden tray to place a jigsaw could be requested during the convalescent period. We had our books and sometimes a comforting drink. If the illness had been prolonged Mum would buy a special treat and we would have a pink pomegranate to pick at, which consumed the long lonely hours of 'being poorly' as the tiny fleshy seeds were extracted from their paper like cells. I crammed a small handful into my mouth, pressed them between my tongue and the roof of my mouth waiting to feel the juices flow as I squeezed them dry. If I squeezed too hard there would be a slightly bitter taste released from the pips.

Boredom usually aided my recovery. Having been deprived of company I couldn't wait to be 'better'. The process of convincing Mum that I wanted to get up was almost more difficult than it had been to convince her that I was not well enough to go to school. She would fetch up the glass thermometer and stick it under my tongue for the allotted three minutes. If it failed to register over 98.4F then I was officially well. I took some perverse delight if she read anything over 100F, for then it proved that, as an invalid, I required one hundred percent attention from her.

"Mmm, I'm not sure if I shook it down enough last time," she would query the result. So the thermometer would receive another severe shake before it was re-inserted and my temperature taken again.

I did manage to get chicken pox from other children and then just as I was recovering a fresh amount of spots appeared. Dr Richie was called to the house and confirmed that I had contracted measles. I had quite enjoyed being ill with chicken pox, apart from the itchy spots that had been coated in white Calamine lotion, as I didn't really feel unwell. I had been able to enjoy some new Rupert annuals and some jigsaws so had been kept quite amused, but the measles had brought with it a high temperature and feeling very poorly. I just wanted to sleep.

Dad did not like us missing school. If signs of recovery could be seen he expected us to be back at school.

"A cold isn't an illness" he would proclaim. "It's just a cold." He suffered with a bad back all his working life but never admitted to feeling under the weather even when his sharp temper signalled that he was not well. As a child he had contracted Scarlet Fever and Rheumatic fever and had spent two years lying in a hospital bed.

"If you're well enough to be up and about then you're well enough for school." Losing so much of his own schooling he didn't want us to do the same.

"If you educate a man, you educate a man; but if you educate a woman you educate a family" was his favourite homily. He had high expectations for his daughters. As he was always inquisitive and resourceful so he expected us to make something of ourselves.

We didn't have a classical music background and our general knowledge, such as it was, was gleaned from the set of encyclopaedias in the front room or from the local library. I had little interest in non-fiction books. Dad enjoyed brass bands probably from his childhood days and when working for Oakes Colliery in Nottingham. When a piece of classical music came on the wireless I had no informed ear to appreciate the pieces. Dad, for some reason liked and recognised two pieces; the William Tell overture by Rossini and the Redetsky March by Strauss. I always muddled the two pieces up although they were so different. 'Para rum, para rum, para rum, pum pum'.

"Which one is this?" He would fire the question at me when the music was played on the wireless. I attempted a guess which usually resulted in naming the wrong piece causing him to roll his eyes at my stupidity.

I also made the error in innocently asking whether he had fought in the Crimean war instead of the Korean War. Orally the two words sounded very similar. He shook his head at my ignorance. If I became disheartened by not being able to achieve something and blurt out that I couldn't do it, he would explode.

"There's no such thing as can't," he would become exasperated by any sign of defeatism. His Navy days had ensured that he could coax most machinery into action. Not always able to rely on a supply of replacement parts for the ship's engines whilst at war made him very adaptable at 'juggling' various bits and pieces into improvised solutions. He would 'worry' at a problem until he had found an answer. As he set high standards for himself so he felt that we should do the same. Dad deplored the misuse of equipment and we were not allowed to blame shoddy work on anything.

"A poor workman blames his tools." We would be reprimanded.

During one summer we were invited to go and stay for a week's holiday with his sister, Aunt Sally and her husband Marian, up in Nottingham, experiencing a quite different standard of living than we had at home. Their well furnished spacious detached privately owned house in substantial gardens made our council house seem quite humble. Her table would provide sumptuous feasts with plenty for everyone. Our cousin Tadek had a room full of expensive toys, exquisite sailing boats, cameras, telescopes, musical instruments, books, everything that a young boy could desire. We had a lovely time playing Cowboys and Indians 'shooting' at each other with silver guns and able to refill the guns with a seemingly endless supply of ribbon-stripped caps curled up in a cap tin. I got so carried away, sailing his boat on the little stream that edged their garden, thinking it was quite like heaven. Although on one occasion having climbed a tree I slipped out and cracked my head and awoke to find the silver gun still in my hand but trailing in the water.

Usually as Dad worked up until Saturday afternoon we only had one day to be with him and our holidays were limited to day trips to the seaside due to inadequate finances. I would so look forward to the planned outing to Cliftonville, Broadstairs, Folkestone, Dover, Whitstable, Herne Bay or Margate. We would set of with high hopes and sunny skies from the Maidstone West Station. Mum had packed Heinz tomato soup in a flask and bread rolls and plastic beakers. We had boiled egg sandwiches and a thin sponge sandwich cake with home made raspberry jam inside. We were triumphant if we managed to bag an empty carriage, sliding the stiff door open as we jiggled in the corridor before claiming the whole area as our own. Sitting by the window I watched the smoke from the steam engine waft past as the chatter of the wheels rumbled over the track. "We're on our way; we're on our way' they clicked and clacked. We had packed our buckets and spades, our swimming costumes, towels and spare vest and knickers, 'just in case'.

Gradually as the view changed from looking at the backs of houses to open fields, the sky began to darken as tiny spots of rain streaked the carriage windows. Mum saw our disappointed faces as the view became obscured by the build up of condensation.

"It might just be a passing shower."

But the rain became relentless. We had packed our transparent plastic macs with hoods and rubber buttons. Making our way from the station we walked against the rain towards the beach. Other day trippers had found some respite from the driving rain inside a bus shelter. We walked up and down to find some similar accommodation. Finally we found a bench inside. Mum decided that it was time for lunch. She poured the hot soup into our beakers and we warmed our hands as we sipped the soup.

"Sandwich anyone?" We greedily devoured the food and waited for the rain to pass. Eventually the weather took pity on us and the rain clouds partially lifted. Trouping down to the beach we set Mum, still in her coat, upon the plastic macs together with the paraphernalia of towels and bags, and started to help Dad build a sandcastle before the sea came in. The damp sand was perfect for constructing walls and turrets, towers and moats. We dug sand and tipped it out for Dad, the grand architect, as he constructed the castle. He drew more plans for defence walls in the sand and we were allowed to build the outer walls, leaving him to fashion the more delicate castellation. The afternoon wore on and we became so absorbed by the work that we were surprised to find that a few curious holiday makers had come to look at our workmanship. We had brought some little flags to decorate the turrets. Mum had her brownie camera and a photograph was taken of us all sitting inside the outer defences, Mum still in her coat and Dad wearing his 'cricket' shoes.

Although the day had not gone as expected; the baggy swimming costumes were still wrapped inside the towels, we caught the train back quite happily after we had waited to see the castle 'stormed' by the sea as the waves reclaimed the beach.

Most of our neighbours still caught the bus, walked to the local 'top shops', cycled to work, or commuted up to 'the Smoke', working in the city, from the two train stations in Maidstone. They did not go abroad on holiday although some were fortunate enough to be able to stay in a hotel for a week or two, or to go to Butlin's Holiday Camp, but mostly people went on day trips either by coach or train. Further along our road there was a family that did own a car. One day they went out for the day and stopped to have a picnic by the road side. A lorry carrying hot tar crashed and tipped its load over them, killing the wife and the two girls. We read the terrible details of the tragedy in the Kent Messenger.

By the second year at the junior school my standard of work had dropped again down to C grades, although Miss Perkins commented that in English my work was above average for the class. Generally her positive comments seemed to be at odds with her grades, for she further commented that 'she maintains a high standard of spelling and general presentation', that I had 'great sensitivity in art and craft and an appreciation of good standards of workmanship', whatever that meant, and that I had a 'good sense of leadership' in Physical education.

During the week the wireless programmes 'Time and Tune' and 'Singing Together', provided a diet of music; the lyrics being carefully enunciated for each song. We noisily joined in with the 'Jolly Miller' who lived on the River Dee, sang about the many mice who lived in a windmill in old Amsterdam,' going clip clipperty, clop on the stair' and a strange sea shanty piece asking 'Were you ever in Quebec riding on a donkey?' followed with the rousing chorus 'hey ho and away you go, donkey riding, donkey riding, hey ho and away you go riding on a donkey'. It was so different from being home and hearing Lonnie Donegan and his skiffle group asking us 'Does your chewing gum lose it's flavour on the bedpost overnight?', or telling us that 'My old man's a dustman'.

I also enjoyed naming various flowers and plants, collecting the petals and leaves for the nature study project, as my interest in nature grew.

Mum and Dad gave over two areas of the back garden to Heather and me. I loved having the opportunity to plant packets of seeds, watching impatiently for the shoots of the radishes and lettuces to appear through the soil. Gradually as Dad's interest in gardening waned I took over more and more of the back garden. One day close to Mothering Sunday I saw that our neighbour had small clumps of snowdrops flowering under the hedge. I was seized with a desire to have them. Guiltily looking around I thrust my hand under the fence to pick the delicate flowers. Just as I was about to withdraw my hand I glanced up at the front room window. Our neighbour's face looked down on me; she fixed my eyes with her stare, and then very slowly shook her head in reproach. I was mortified. Not only had I stolen the flowers but had been caught in the act. She was not even going to come out to tell me off. I had to slink away from my tail between my legs, my face flushed with embarrassment. I couldn't even give the flowers to Mum as my shame would have been too obvious. I left them in the drawer in my bedroom until they wilted and died.

It was by this time that I decided that my favourite colour was pink. Suddenly I desired a pink lampshade and stand for my bedroom and pestered Mum until she gave in. Next I saw an Aladdin's lamp in garish swirly pink which I also clamoured for until Mum acquiesced to my demand. I used the battery operated lamp to read my story books under the covers when I had been given instructions to put out the light and go to sleep. But how could I sleep when I needed to know what was going to happen next? The lamp would flicker making it difficult to complete each passage, eventually I would be found out and the lamp removed from the bedroom.

By this time I also had a compulsion to learn how to whistle. For days on end I went secretly up the path to the top of the garden, pursed my licked lips together and blew. A faint wheeze came disappointingly out. Finally after so many futile cheek-aching attempts I managed to make an appropriate sound. I practised my new skill around the house driving Mum mad. Next I practised the art of winking and then of raising just one eyebrow quizzically as Dad could do. At first I had to hold one eyebrow down until finally the muscles responded.

Each Christmas Heather and I would stick strip of paper chains together which Dad would then string up from the central ceiling light towards each corner of the room. We would go into the park and collect twigs and springs of holly. Using green crepe paper we would then snip each strip of paper into fringes and wind the fringed crepe around each twig. When all the twigs had been covered we stuck them into a red block of wood that was trimmed with red paper. Mum had some old tree decorations designed with nursery rhymes that we strung around the 'tree' with the finale being the fairy with her lopsided black wig that had become a little detached over the years of sitting astride a tree. Our traditional homemade decorations ensured that the cost of Christmas was kept to a minimum. Dad made us sugar mice with a string tail and after Christmas we would start to munch on them our teeth jarring with the hard rich sweetness; starting at the back of the mouse until only the nose and ears were left. We roasted chestnuts on the fire, which would explode unexpectedly and shower us with pieces of half-cooked, half-raw, nut.

But our greatest treat was to receive a parcel from our Aunty Sally. Her expensive hampers contained food treasures nestling amongst fine straw. We savoured each exotic tin and packet as it was lifted from its straw nest. Tins of ham, red salmon, peaches, a muslin-wrapped Christmas pudding, cakes and biscuits, jars of preserves, and fruits soaked in liqueur lay awaiting discovery. Even the straw hamper itself spoke of luxury; too good to be discarded.

By the third year at the school I had become quite indifferent about my schoolwork. My grades of 'C's and a single 'B' for composition and the 'very good' remarks for the ungraded subjects left me quite cold. Miss Thorogood, the headmistress added her own comment on the report congratulating me on 'good grades' which seemed a nonsense unless it was indeed impossible to gain 'A' grades in that class.

One spring weekend we found out that there was to be a fancy dress competition at the fair over at South Park on the Loose Road. Dad decided that I would make a splendid White Rabbit. He had long had a love affair with Lewis Carol's 'Alice in Wonderland' and 'Through the Looking Glass'. Having acquired a reel-to-reel tape recorder he took great delight in reciting various pieces into the attached microphone. We would have to listen to his rendition of, 'You are old, father William', the 'Jabberwocky' and Tweedledee's, 'The sun was shining on the Sea', with each recitation seeming more lengthy than the one before.

That afternoon he made me a pair of long ears that were attached to an old woollen balaclava hood and a large cardboard clock, I had an old jacket of his that reached my knees but he wanted me to have white leggings. Mum found an old pair of thick woollen stockings that she tried to dye white. Unfortunately the task had been started too late that morning and the stockings were still wet and mainly greyish. I had to endure a damp bus journey being stared at by the other curious, faintly amused, passengers. I didn't win a prize but had a commendation for effort since I made the judge smile by baring my lips, attempting to imitate a rabbit by showing him my protruding teeth. In the final year I found myself in Miss Fisher's class. She was an Amazon of a woman with a cheerful disposition. Encouraging all aspects of PE she took the class on the bus down to town for our swimming lessons in the Victorian style Maidstone Baths. I liked her. She awarded me a 'B+' for my reading, a 'B–', for my composition, but a disastrous 'D+' for my spelling. Her remarks were more than generous.

'Julia reads widely, and consequently her English work has benefited. Her written work is usually of a very high and mature standard and she has produced a good year's work. Her spelling varies'.

Her general remarks found that I was, 'a very mature, helpful and friendly member of the form. She has worked very hard throughout the year at a very mature level. She has a very inquiring mind, and will not be content until she has reasoned out exactly why certain things are so. Julia's art and craft and needlework are excellently done and this artistic tendency should be encouraged. Julia has worked hard in PE and games but particularly with her swimming.'

Maidstone Swimming baths were very antiquated. The red brick built Victorian baths had once been used by the public in taking a bath as many houses did not have any bathing facilities. Inside there were high diving platforms accessed by steep slippery metal steps at the deep end and smaller steps at the shallow end of the tiled pool. Each tiny changing cubicle had a ragged oilskin cloth draped across the entrance which afforded very little privacy to those changing inside and due to the height of the curtain those who chose to sit on the balcony upstairs could see into each one from their high vantage point. You had to duck down in the cramped cubicle which you had to share with another child. Unfortunately the curtain was also too short which meant that swimmers in the pool could, if they swam close enough to the edge, also peer up and see exposed limbs or more depending on the state of the dilapidated screen. It was hard enough to get undressed but getting dry and dressed again presented a greater challenge. The baggy costume had to be peeled away from wet skin; reluctant to be parted from its occupant and then the obligatory tight rubber swimming cap wrenched off leaving a tell-tale red line across our foreheads. Then we had to attempt to towel ourselves dry without knocking into each other and finally there was the race to the bus as we were always running out of time. So many times during that term we had to have plasters applied to our feet due to the prevalence of verrucas. Once we had waded through the foot bath we would line up for our upturned feet to be inspected for tell-tale black pin-prick spots before entering the water.

Back at school Miss Fisher would set us gymnastic challenges. We would launch ourselves high into the air from wooden boxes onto thin rubber matting remembering to "bend your knees" on landing. She would assist the descent holding onto our arms and lifting us whooshing back into the air again with a triumphant "well done!"

For the class outing we went up to London to the V&A Museum. A coach arrived at the school and we clambered aboard. I thought that it was going to be quite dull, a bit like Maidstone Museum, until we glimpsed into each small room, each set in a different period of time. I was fascinated. We started in the early eighteen century, progressed to the Victorian era and when we came to the 'lounge of the 1940's' I realised that I was looking at a combination of Gran's house and our own front room. For the first time I realised that history was a part of me. It was quite thrilling. We peeped at the 1940's kitchen; there was a replica of our cooker with its Queen Anne splayed legs that Dad joked about. "That's due to all those heavy cakes your mother bakes!" Then there were Gran's painted green and cream kitchen cupboards, her bathroom geyser, her brown Bakelite light switches with the small rounded metal switch in the centre and her two pin electric sockets. On a low table sat our Bakelite wireless together with our half moon rug, surrounded by square chairs placed in front of the coal fire with the fire tongs and coal bucket at one side.

It was around this time Dad had decided that we were old enough to be introduced to archery. He set about making a set of bows and arrows for us. Using wood from a willow tree for the bows he joined and glued thin strips together testing for their strength and flexibility. Our arrows had fine sharp tips of brass and the flight feathers were coloured coded so that we could recognise our own set. We would set off across the park and select a tree and then Dad would pace back to an appropriate spot that would present a challenge to our skills to hit the 'target'. Taking turns we aimed at the tree trunk; the tipped arrows thudded into the wood, stuck fast in the tree. When we had shown some prowess we would then play the game. Two of us would go off and then the 'hunter' armed with a staff would attempt to find his quarry. There was a specially selected large tree trunk that had been sawn off at its base that was designated as the HQ. The aim of the game was for the 'hunted' to manage to get back to the HQ without being spotted. At first a hiding place had to be found. This could be up a tree or in a dip of land.

One day we were close to the lake and saw some soldiers from Maidstone barracks 'on manoeuvres'. They hadn't spotted us as they snaked and crawled their way towards us. Dad beckoned for us to remain in hiding. Their progress was painfully slow and although they were attempting to 'lay low' to prevent detection from our vantage point they looked extremely vulnerable having taken no attempt to find bushes and trees in which to hide. They looked faintly ridiculous to us. Our plan was to wait until they were close enough; then fire our arrows across their path to show that they had been exposed to the 'enemy', which was us. Finally Dad looked at his watch and realised that we could wait no longer. We just had to fire our arrows towards the spot that they would have advanced to then walk calmly out from behind the tree, retrieved our arrows and walked home. I had wanted to have been close enough to see their surprise at the 'ambush' but it was not to be.

On Sundays Heather and I would also be sent down the town to the Baptist Church in Knightrider Street to attend the Sunday school, kitted out in obligatory white gloves. I'm not sure why we continued to attend that church in preference to the new one on the Shepway Estate. Whatever the reason, I disliked the idea of having to go, but once there thoroughly enjoyed listening to the Bible stories from the Old and New Testament. After the Sunday school session we would be lead down the stairs and into the main part of the church. I was quite fascinated by the Baptism pool at the front of the church wondering if people who were baptised as adults had to go in fully clothed, and whether the water was heated for that eventuality.

For harvest festivals Mum would send us off each carrying a small box of fruit. Our offering was quite meagre compared to other children but we were still taken to the altar to place our box with the other abundance of fruit and vegetables. Pride of place was reserved for a magnificent bread loaf shaped as a sheath of corn. It was a beautiful display. Food was then distributed to the 'Poor of the Borough' although I never knew who they were. I think that we always took a sixpence for the church funds each week to put onto the wooden collection plate.

Heather also was allowed to go to the Saturday cinema at the Granada situated on the corner of Stone Street and Knightrider Street. How I envied her independence. But strangely when I was older I still never went; perhaps they had stopped the performances for children by then. However on a Thursdays afternoons, after school had finished, the pupils at the Junior School were able to attend a film show for a small price. How I wept to see plucky, resourceful Lassie overcoming all obstacles; often at the mercy of dastardly villains and complicated conspiracies but still able to defeat them all; romping home to a hero's welcome. Flickering black and white images shown on a large canvas screen held me entranced as we sat cross-legged on the large hall floor, and I loved Lady and the Tramp that was shown in glorious Technicolor.

Dad was given an old projector and lovingly coaxed it back to life. He hung an old bed sheet on the curtain track in the front room and we had our own show, watching borrowed films and clips from the Model Railway enthusiasts. The old flickering films showed some damage but we still eagerly watched the scratched frames counting down '4, 3,

2, and picture!' and were sad when the reel finished and repeatedly flicked the last strip of film against the spool.

Around this time Mum realised that she needed to take up some part time work, for as Dad said, "There's always too much week left at the end of the money".

When she had heard that a lady living in a big house down in Willington Street could offer her some domestic work she put the proposition to him. At first he was adamant that she should stay at home and not take the job. Although he had some enlightened views, his childhood in Nottingham had reinforced a belief that the man of the house should be the breadwinner and provider for his family. He would not hear of it. Eventually she won the argument.

As she would not always be at home during the lunch hour I was to have school dinners. I missed skipping down the road during the dinner break but the meals were quite a novelty at first and then I got used to the routine. Some teachers watched to see that we ate up every scrap to keep the waste for the pig bins at a minimum. If we were particularly slow then we would sit in the deserted dinning room until the plate had been cleared to their satisfaction. I was not a fussy eater but found the powdered mashed potato quite difficult at times especially when it contained the lumps of dry powder not mixed in.

Perhaps the rows started then or perhaps they had been brewing for some time and I had not noticed them. Sundays were the worst. There would be mutterings and grumbles which escalated as the morning wore on. Dad usually went over the park to his Model Engineers Society where they had a circular stone track to run the model steam trains that they built. I didn't like to listen and tried to blot out the words. The frustration in his voice grew and the row got louder until Mum would eventually answer back. When we went downstairs she would be flustering in the kitchen looking pinched and hurt. Dad would then realise that he had gone too far and attempt to make it up with her. He would give us a guilty wink and go into the kitchen to soothe her. She was slow to anger but once roused she managed to subdue his shouts and bluster. He knew that she had an inner strength and that for all his raging trying to impose his will she would stick her heels in and bide her time.

On the Sundays when he stayed at home we listened to the wireless, laughing at our favourite programmes: The Clitheroe Kid, The Glums with Ron and Eth, the saucy Round the Horne, Hancock's Half Hour and The Navy Lark featuring Heather Chase and Leslie Philips whilst Mum clattered in the kitchen preparing a roast dinner with the usual scraggy ribbed breast of lamb.

Dad's interests rarely included her. They lived side by side living their own lives sometimes quite separately. He would be devising his next project, shaping a set of bows and arrows for us, constructing a miniature theatre stage, whilst she would be immersed in her cooking, allowing us to play without fuss, although she was ever attentive to our needs and demands. Once, when attending a Mother's Union group meeting she found out that unmarried mothers were unable to join and came back home bristling with indignation, finding the ruling quite offensive and 'un Christian'.

"They need more support than the rest of us," she declared.

In the evenings after the family dinner Dad would disappear outside to his workshop and Mum would be left to do the dishes. We would hear his humming lathe, cutting, grinding and shrieking into lumps of metal as he fashioned the next part for his engine. His shed was a room of ordered chaos. On the wooden bench taking pride of place was fastened his lathe with looping leather drive belts above the lathe bed. Pieces of spiralled shiny yellow brass, amber copper and coils of razor-sharp silver steel rejected from the rotating blades would festoon the bench and floor. There were labelled jars of screws, nails, nuts and bolts, pins, ball bearings and all manner of oil, paint, white spirit bottles and tins lining the shelves. In half open drawers and around the work surface he had an array of saws, files, hammers, mallets, box planes, taps and dies, screwdrivers, spanners, enough to keep a small shop in stock. All had their place; he could lay his hand on anything that he wanted. But to us it looked as if someone had come into the shed and thrown everything up in the air and the equipment and tools had landed and stayed where they fell. In one corner of the dusty, cobwebbed corner Dad teased me about his pet spider Charlie. Charlie lived in a tunnelled web. Dad swore that Charlie would come out and stay watching him whilst he worked to keep him company. In the summer Dad also said that he would swat an unsuspecting fly onto the web for Charlie to eat and that the spider would run out, seize it and rush back into his web.

On warmer evenings he would draw up a high wooden stool for me and I was allowed to watch as his graceful hands, hardened by work, would fasten a cylinder of metal so that it could be turned and cut into the required shape. As the metal heated with the friction of the cutting blade so he would drizzle a cooling white liquid over the piece. We sat together both watching the bright slivers of metal cascade over the bench. There was no conversation. I was expected to sit quietly whilst he worked. His pipe somehow stayed put, gripped lightly between his teeth, occasionally billowing with a puff of smoke. Sometimes a small spark of fire and ash would fall onto his dark blue working jacket. He would scrape out the rest of the ash from the bowl of the pipe with his penknife and proceed to pull long fibres of tobacco from his Erinmore Mixture tin. When it got too cold or I had watched for long enough I would slip off the stool and run back into the house my clothes holding on to the smell of his pipe smoke.

It was around this time that Dad acquired a Bella motor scooter. He had had the long walk to work prior to this acquisition. The bike had a large metal yellow daisy badge attached to the front. On a Saturday afternoon he would allow me to ride pillion we would whizz along Plains Avenue to Gran's house. She had bought a television set. Finally I could watch What's my Line?, Sooty and Sweep, and Robin Hood with its memorable signature tune,

Robin Hood Robin Hood riding through the glen,
Robin Hood Robin Hood with his band of men,
Feared by the bad; loved by the good,
Robin Hood, Robin Hood, Robin Hood.

Then there was Crackerjack, Champion the Wonder Horse, Lenny the Lion, The Black and White Minstrel Show or the Billy Cotton Band Show with his welcoming call, "wakey wake ee". We would set off with me tightly hugging his waist. It became quite a habit that we would watch the afternoon programmes, have a cup of tea and then whizz off back home.

A few years later Dad was giving a lift to a work mate one evening. It was a wet night and the rain was pouring down. The traffic lights in town had just turned to green as he approached, but as he was about to accelerate, a hooded pedestrian stepped off the kerb into the road in front of him. Dad applied his brakes to avoid him, but at the same time his pillion passenger took fright at what he thought was going to happen, and leapt off the bike causing it to slew around on the road. Dad was left trapped under the bike unable to move at first. As he became aware of where he was he stared down at his legs and realised that his foot was not pointing the right way and so straightened his leg. At the hospital a weary doctor, who had been attending to the carnage of a previous fatal motorbike accident prior to Dad's arrival, took one look at him and pronounced him fit enough to go home. It was later that night that Dad's knee began to swell. During that night he started to hallucinate, shouting about the bloody hands on the deck of the ship; that sailors were drowning in the burning sea. They were screaming for help but were helplessly caught in the oil and fire.

In the morning he pulled back the covers and we looked at his knee. A huge livid purple swelling covered most of his bloated leg. Mum called the doctor. He took one look and referred him back to the hospital. Dad arrived back home, his leg encased in a plaster cast that went from the top of his thigh down to his ankle. They had realised that his knee had been badly dislocated.

Some weeks later when they removed the plaster Dad found that he had little stability in the leg; when stepping back it would suddenly give way. He returned to the hospital and this time they informed him that due to him not having been properly examined at the time of the accident he had indeed dislocated his knee but had torn all the ligaments that held the knee joint in place. As so much time had passed by, these would no longer knit back together. He would always limp. The limp exasperated the continuous pain of his bad back but he never took time off work; his ill temper and asking for some aspirins were the only indication that he felt so bad. For him it would be giving in, somehow showing a weakness. Besides he would never let the owner of the mill, Major Pitt, down. Major Pitt relied on 'Jack' to fix things. In later years when a telephone was provided for Dad so that he could be called out, Dad would trudge through the thick snow across Mote Park to reach the mill if the roads were impassable. Dad knew where the sluice gates were from the River Len down to the River Medway, to avoid any flooding. He would crawl through barely cooled boilers to assess the damage to the machinery, and never doubted that Major Pitt would look after him giving his loyalty to a mill that was struggling to compete in the paper industry despite the 'Rumours'.

We were given fine sheets of handmade paper for our paintings and drawings with instructions not to waste it. Dad would proudly hold the paper up to the light so that we could read the water mark.

"This paper will never go yellow." he would proudly boast. "Not like the machine rubbish that they make these days". He told us tales of how a mix-up had occurred, with a Sharp's consignment of gelatine being delivered to them in error whilst their gelatine had ended up at the toffee factory.

"We couldn't make paper with their rubbish, but they could make toffee with ours!" he boosted proudly.

At home we still had the most basic gadgets but Mum did buy a pressure cooker. It came into its own by making the cheapest cuts of meat tender and tasty, but it emitted the most frightening amount of steam prior to the pressure being released. One day the valve must have malfunctioned or Mum might have forgotten to turn the electric plate setting down. The next moment the pressure cap blew off spraying lamb stew over the kitchen walls and ceiling.

Our diet was still restricted by money shortages. More than not when coming home 'famished' from school I would resort to raiding the pantry and spread thick waxy white dripping on a thick slice of bread to fill me up. We would have to wait until Dad arrived home from work so that we would eat together as a family. Our job was to set the table with the tablecloth, cutlery and serviettes and then assist Mum in the kitchen. Sometimes it would be stirring the gravy to prevent lumps forming. I would try to tell her what I had been doing during the day but she was more often than not too flustered and engrossed with her cooking and only had half an ear for me. I would read something out that I had composed at school; some half-completed story to see what she thought of it. Half way through a sentence I would realise that she wasn't paying any attention to the plot.

"...and so once they had gone to........." I finished in mid flow and asked "What do you think Mum?"

"oh, mm, very nice Julie, now where did I put that strainer?"

I don't know why I persisted in the charade knowing that it would be the same each time.

"You never listen to my stories; I don't know why I even bother!" I flounced out of the kitchen and stamped upstairs.

"You can see that I'm busy!" her voice followed me as I reached the landing, but I was not to be pacified. I wanted her praise and admiration but it was not to be.

Another time I was so overcome with exasperation that I took hold of the paper and tore it into shreds. "There's no point in doing anything! I shouted in temper, "Look what you have made me do!"

"I don't know what has got into you these days Julie," her hurt voice provoked shame at my petulance. "You never used to have such a temper."

I decided that I would stay up in my room denying them my company, but hunger always managed to break my resolve so I had to join them at the table whilst still trying to maintain an air of hurt indifference and disapproval.

At that time I had also acquired new skills taking up with the latest craze of playing 'two-ball' against the coal shed wall. It drove the neighbours mad as my first attempts meant a ball escaping into their garden on a regular basis. At first throwing the two rubber balls in rotation was difficult but as my dexterity improved so I managed three and then finally managed four. It was a kind of juggling against the wall. All the girls played with them, chanting various sing-song verses to go with each turn.

We mastered the art of 'cats cradle' winding our fingers around the string to create 'named' patterns and shapes. The bright coloured plastic hoola hoops took our fancy next as we gyrated the hoop around our waists until we could almost keep it in place with just an imperceptible rock of our hips moving back and forth. I also had a set of Jacks. We would bounce the small rubber ball high into the air, which allowed us time to pick up first one jack at a time until all had been gathered up. The next part of the game meant two jacks to be collected at a time, then three until the final throw had to be a little higher to allow sufficient time for all five jacks to be collected at once. With that section of the game completed we then had different trials. One was called 'caves'. We had to coax each jack into a cave. One hand curved round to resemble a cave mouth by setting the small finger side down on the ground with the thumb and index finger becoming the opening to the cave. Our other hand would then have to throw the ball up and whilst the ball was in the air use the same hand and attempt to push the jacks towards the mouth of the cave until all jacks were inside.

Mum didn't know that we also dare-devilled each other to see it we could not only walk along the top of the narrow stone park wall but also to skip along it. Then we would see if we could jump from the wall onto the green metal electric sub-station box and back again, knowing that there was a ten to twelve foot drop below us. In the summer the metal box retained the burning heat of the sun which made any landing and possible sitting down on the top quite uncomfortable.

Although there were very few cars or lorries driving through our estate our road afforded a quick route from Loose Road to the main Ashford Road at the end of Willington Street if the driver wanted to miss out the town. It was still a novelty for us to watch the cars pass by and then the craze of collecting car registration numbers started. We scribbled on little bits of paper the numbers and then did comparisons at the end of the afternoon to see who had managed to collect the most numbers. Stephanie's brother,Stuart, always amassed an enviable amount of numbers and had piles of notepads which he kept at home It never occurred to me to make numbers up and I think that I had a form of dyslexia with numbers and letters that had no meaning. I could read sentences in a blink of an eye but trying to copy a sequence of letters and numbers from the registration plate just defeated me. It was a game that I soon gave up on.

One summer Gran's stomach pains got so bad that she was finally referred to the hospital. For years she had rubbed on liniment and taken aspirin for the pain and sleeping pills for her disturbed nights. The hospital found that she had a fistula in her bowel which would necessitate an operation. She had to have part of the colon removed and have a temporary colostomy bag. If the operation was successful she would then go back in to have the colon rejoined and the colostomy bag removed. It was decided that she needed to have someone to look after her and so Gran came to stay with us for a few months. I can still recall the gut-wrenching smell when the colostomy bag had to be emptied, and cream applied around the open wound to prevent soreness and infection. Poor Mum had clean up the toilet and bathroom after frequent 'accidents' occurred. We were so glad when she had the second operation and was fit to return home.

Apart from visiting relatives and Mum's two school friends Joan Sharp and Gwen Cotton, we rarely had anyone visiting our house except for Gran. It began to occur to me that as a family we kept very much to ourselves. We didn't have transport and so relied on the bus or train for family outings. Dad's sister Sally and her son Tadek would come down from Nottingham once in a blue moon but otherwise our little family had little social contact. Being so insular made me hungry for outings and mixing with other people but also quite inept at knowing how to mix. Whenever we visited Dad on a Sunday afternoon when the model railway was running the trains for the public I always felt awkward and shy. I didn't know how to respond appropriately to ordinary greetings from the other adults. One day there was a lady, whom I hadn't met before, sitting on the bench at the 'station' contentedly chatting away to another member of the Society. Immediately I was captivated by her easy conversation and good humour. Her conversation was peppered with interesting anecdotes and amusing incidents. I wanted to stay at her feet listening to the fluidity of words tumbling from her. I must have presented an odd figure, not speaking, just a mute lump, gazing up at her in adoration.

It was the power of words that took me to places that I wanted to stay. But equally this desire to be enchanted by the written word caused much anguish for my Mum. On the occasions when she had to 'pop out' leaving me with instructions to attend to certain matters I would mechanically answer quite appropriately without knowing what she had said. I would then 'come to' after a length of time only to realise that I didn't know where she was or what she had expected me to do. On one occasion she had asked me to keep an eye on some potatoes that she had put in the oven to bake. As usual I had said that, "yes I would look check to see when they had been done', which was quite vital as our oven had no temperature control, just a thin glass thermometer on the outside door which showed how hot the oven was inside. The only way to maintain a certain temperature was to turn it on and off at regular intervals. I went upstairs and found an Ian Fleming book in Heather's bedroom. Firstly I shouldn't have been prying in her room and secondly I shouldn't have taken the book but I seized upon it and started reading. It was sometime later that I became aware of the smoke swirling up the stairs. In panic I flew down two at a time to find the smoke filled kitchen. I threw open the back door to try and clear the air before opening the oven door. Inside the oven were the charred remains of the potatoes, resembling little lumps of coke.

In all families there are family sayings and references only known and understood by the family members. In our family Dad repeated snatches of old music hall pieces, full of naughty innuendo, and used numerous nautical references which we in turn adopted.

"I put my finger in a woodpecker's hole
the woodpecker said 'well bless my soul
take it out!
take it out!
remove it'."

"Amos! " Mum would attempt to admonish him half-heartedly, as we giggled at his crafty wink.

He would ask us to 'free the slide' which meant that he wanted you to pass the butter. We learnt to tidy up after he requested that we 'cleared the decks' and 'stow things away,' so we got things 'ship shape' and knew that space was tight when he said that there wasn't room to 'swing a cat', that he would have a smoke on his pipe 'when the sun comes up over the yard arm', or that a particularly cold day would be 'brass monkey' weather. And we knew exactly where he was going when he said that he had to 'water the horses' or 'pay a call', and giggled uncontrollably when he loudly farted and then, acting as if the noise had surprised him, would say in a mincing tone, "pardon me vicar!" If he was particularly full after a meal he would pat his stomach and say in a satisfied tone, "well I feel like a pregnant earwig," or "I'm as fat as a NAAFI cat." And if we were out walking and he saw a greyhound walking with its master we would wait for the inevitable remark, "there goes another racing pilchard."

When we went to visit Cranbrook we would pass Goudhurst on the way, with an antique shop on the corner, and again we waited for his usual comment, "I see the 'ante- cue' shop is still doing well!"

As he had been stationed out in Egypt in Alexander for a time during the war he picked up a smattering of Arabic. During our tea he would ask for the 'zibda', and we would pass the butter. And if we asked to do something later he would shrug and say, ' bukra fil mesh mesh', which he said translated roughly as, 'later in the season when the apricots are out', would thank us with, 'shukran' or ask to have a 'shoofti' which meant, to have a look. Our mode of speech and accent was affected by Dad's Derbyshire upbringing and Mum's quiet tone and to some extent our family's isolation. On the bus to Maidstone the chattering women's voices, seemed to my ear, to be very different; their lack of consonants and extended vowels interested me as did their easy familiarity with one another. They greeted each other as long lost friends, asked after each other's spouses or children and gossiped about the latest scandal or rumour. I didn't feel part of their world although we were living on the same council estate, in the same town.

We, as children, identified areas of particular deprivation according to the state of front gardens, discarded toys, piled up rubbish, garden gates hanging on their hinges and the number of flaxen-haired children viewing you with menace and suspicion as you passed by; Mangravet had a 'bad reputation, as did Tovil and parts of the Foster Clark Estate. At our end of Plains Avenue small gangs of youths would stand together, their numbers providing bravado for them and fear for us. There was no way that the correct response could be given to those who were 'looking for trouble' so we learnt to get past as quickly as possible.

If you did meet their eye they would shout, "Wotcher looking at!" but if you attempted to avoid eye contact the mocking challenge would follow.

"Whatsa matter stuck up cow?"

You were damned either way; they triumphed in their power to intimidate; revelling in our discomfort.

On the bus to town Mum would ask the bus conductor for 'one and a half, return please'. We used to plead to get a seat upstairs so that we could view the whole journey with a bird's eye view, peering into gardens and shops and watching the people get on and off the bus. In the build up to Christmas we would compete to see who could count the most decorated Christmas trees in the windows. The bus conductor would wind the grey ticket machine dials to the correct position and reels of tickets would cascade out. He would hand the small change due to Mum, taking out the coins that had been fed into the columns of the coin machine, resembling a bulky set of Pan's pipes, which was also slung around his neck. On crowded Tuesdays he would struggle to reach all the passengers before they got off at their stop, and have to lift the two machines up in the air to prevent those standing in the aisles catching themselves on the protruding metal. We would hear his voice sing-songing his way down the bus, "anymore fares please, anymore fares?"

It was the trolley bus rides that ran from Loose Valley, down Stone Street and into the town that provided more entertainment. On rainy days white sparks flew from the overhead cables, the windows would steam up and we would be held together in the damp; umbrellas dripping, creating little streams on the black ribbed floor. I loved to press the red rubber bell to tell the driver that it was our stop 'Ding, Ding!'

Tuesdays were busy because it was market day. People thronged over the bridge crossing the River Medway to shop amongst the crowded stalls. I hated Maidstone when Fremlins Brewery down Pudding Lane by Earl Street were brewing their ale. An acrid smell of hops pervaded the whole town.

At Christmas the two prestigious department stores Chiesemans and Dunnings had Father Christmas Grottos; their shop windows beautifully dressed with ever changing artistic displays. To clamber aboard a 'train' and enter the grotto was to embark on a world of fantasy; at each turn of the 'tunnel' a new tableau would enchant. Elves would be figured bending over workbenches fashioning toys; the snow woodland scene would contain endearing dapple-backed deer and wide-eyed rabbits watching from their burrows or shyly peeping from behind trees. There was the desire to press on to reach Father Christmas but then not to go too fast and miss each detail of the wonderful scenes.

At Easter the shops would compete to create sumptuous Spring displays, with trees in a profusion of pink blossom, flowers fashioned amongst the grasses, and rabbits in checked costumes and bonnets holding baskets of brightly wrapped Easter eggs. Window shopping provided a child's delight; they welcomed our attention. In the summer the slim models in swimsuits, sunhats and dark sunglasses would loll in striped deckchairs as model children played with their buckets and spades on the sandy beach lapped by a blue silk sea against a painted backdrop of sun and seagulls. No wonder Heather, with her artistic talents, wanted to become a window dresser; the attention to detail was superb.

Most of our Saturday morning journeys to town however involved food shopping or purchasing household products so I would be dragged past the windows as Mum raced against time to get the shopping over and done with. We bought our vegetables from the Payne's stall in Pudding Lane, our unsliced bread loaves from a bakery in Week Street and our fresh fish, copiously wrapped in white waxed paper, from the cavernous shop in Earl Street. Mum and I loved kippers, which the rest of our family loathed, and she would buy a pair for a treat for us to share on Saturday. We got the meat from David Greigs or Betts the butchers, and various odd household bits and pieces from Woolies. At Paynes' shop most of the fruit and vegetables spilled out onto the street in boxes displayed to their best advantage. The best and most desirable to tempt the shopper sat at the front. But whenever Mum asked for some apples, oranges, tomatoes or onions the shop assistant would invariably take a brown bag and furtively throw in a selection from behind the counter, twirling up the two ends of the bag to resemble two ears. When we got home and she opened up the bags she would often exclaim at the poor quality of the produce.

"That's the last time I go there!" But she never went anywhere else and never asked to see the fruit and vegetables before they were bagged up.

Our shoes were mended at the cobblers, "we'll just have the heels done as it will be cheaper than having the soles done as well," and bought from new at the Golden Boot shop at the top of Gabriel's Hill. We always had to have 'sensible' Clarks' brown leather sandals for the summer and equally 'sensible' shoes with laces for the winter. The delight of having my feet measured on the metal plate and having the metal bar slid down until it met my toes was tempered by the fact that all the shoes that I liked in the shop window were not going to be the ones that were finally purchased. I longed to have white lace trimmed ankle socks and pretty fashionable shoes with bows and buckles but Mum was adamant and there was no point arguing.

"You'll thank me for it one day when all these other girls end up with bad feet and bunions."

We trudged around the town with the heavy shopping bags sometimes having to return in the afternoon as we couldn't carry it all in one go. We never went into some of the high class shops. Blakes in the High Street was particularly forbidding; the window displays showed women in 'fuddy-duddy' jackets and twin sets, evening gowns and hats. Visiting Featherstone's in Earl Street was quite a treat. It had 'Heath Robinson' cables stretching across the ceiling and cylindrical tubes that could be opened by the cashier so that she could place the money inside. It would whoosh up and off to another part of the store and then whoosh back again with the change and bill of sale inside. I was fascinated by the contraption.

During the one holiday we went to visit Knole Park. I remember being enchanted as the deer in the park came up close to us to see if we any food to feed them.

And so my junior school days wore on. I began to pick up tales about other children being promised a new bike if they could pass the 11 plus and go to the Grammar School. As I didn't have an 'old' bike I knew a new one was completely out of the question. My friend Heather Lewis had a lovely bike and would sometimes bring it down with her to play with me. I would have to wait impatiently for a 'turn' which she reluctantly allow me to have after she had ridden up and down the road; seemingly for most of the afternoon. I hated myself for wanting it so much and for letting her know how much it meant to me. "My turn now," she would announce after a ridiculous few moments. And I had to acquiesce as I knew that she could deny me at any time. I had hardly managed to master the skill of staying on the saddle without wobbling before she then tired of the game and went home.

As Mum was working more hours cleaning and spending time at Gran's, helping her out, I had more time at home left to my own devices. Strict instructions about chores and duties were left for me but more often than not I chose to ignore them. During a half term break from school I was bored and fretted to have some company. Although I had been told to stay in for some purpose I could hear the sound of drilling outside. Intrigued I looked out and saw some children gathered around some workmen who were repairing the road. Within a few moments I joined them. They bantered with the nosey children and stupidly I wanted to show off. Running back across the road I tripped and landed with a thwack against the kerb. Too embarrassed to care about any possible injury I dusted down my skirt and attempted to look nonchalant until I my friend's eyes grew round as she to pointed at my face, "Oh Julie!"

"What's the matter?" Her look started to frighten me.

"It's your tooth!"

"My tooth?" I didn't understand.

You've broken it!"

My hand flew up to feel my mouth. Strange, I could still feel both front teeth although one seemed a little rough.

The workmen stopped to watch. "Now you'll catch it!"

Why did I to come out to play? My thoughts were full of what Mum would say, rather than worrying about the tooth, but that was before I rushed back indoors to examine the damage. Running up the stairs I looked into the small bathroom cabinet mirror. My throat contracted and I could feel my heart thumping. Half the tooth was missing. I just had a triangular piece left. There was no disguising it and Mum would find out that I had disobeyed her.

She arrived home. I waited until she had put her bags heavily down on the kitchen table.

My fingers lingered over my lips as I tried to think what to say. How to explain without rousing a storm?

She looked up sensing that something was amiss, "what's the matter?"

"Oh" I began feebly "I fell over."

"And?"

"Ermm"I reluctantly moved my finger away from my lips to show her. "I broke a bit of my tooth"

I heard her sharp intake of breath.

"Julie!"

My tears started to fall. Sorry for myself, frightened at what she would do or say next.

"And did you go out to play when I told you not to?"

I nodded, not able to speak.

"You are a naughty girl! Now that's what happens when you don't do as you are told!"

"It's only a bit of the tooth." I attempted to pacify her.

"A bit! Well it's not going to grow again you silly girl."

She took me to the National Health dentist who just shrugged and said that it would be fine. Mum didn't question his decision. After nearly a year had passed I woke up with an agonising pain. The tooth, not being capped to protect the nerve, had decayed.

The dentist took the tooth out. I spent the rest of my childhood and twenty years of adulthood resentfully wearing a plate with one false tooth attached.

"That'll teach you to take chunks out of the pavement" My Dad attempted, unsuccessfully, to tease me out of the doldrums.

The false tooth became the bane of my life. I had never felt pretty; being so dowdy and badly dressed and so the pink plastic plate confirmed my conviction, I now certainly never would be. Looking in the mirror I could also see that I was getting fatter. Some called it puppy fat but to me it just looked like fat. I now had hand-me-down clothes from other sources outside the family but found that I seemed to be constantly outgrowing them. It didn't help when my Uncle Marian accompanied Dad's sister Sally on a rare visit to us one summer decided to put me straight. He took one look at me and said that I needed to watch my weight otherwise I would end up 'like a barrel on two legs'. The image was shocking and I was mortified. I also hated my thin hair that always became lanky within a couple of days after washing it. Mum refused to let me wash it more often as she said that it was 'bad for the hair'. Sometimes she relented I was allowed to use a 'dry shampoo'; a powder that could be combed through. It made no different to my rats tails just making it smell rather peculiar. Heather had always had her long hair plaited and 'created' when Mum washed it for her. Mum would come down the stairs after a 'bout' with Heather looking pink and harassed. When I pleaded to have my hair longer she was adamant.

"I've had enough with Heather and her ways!"

I was dragged unwillingly to the hairdressers at regular intervals. I hated the results. Cut to one length straight across the back without any layering or shaping, my thin hair looked, if anything, worse than before. Despite Mum insisting that they would only cut off "an inch or so", the amount of hair to be swept up after the cut denied that that was the case.

"They never do as you ask!" I would explode in frustration. "When I grow up I shall grow it long."

"When you grow up you can!"

"I look horrible!"

"Don't go on so!"

The quarrel continued all the way home. Perhaps it was in that year that I started to lose confidence in myself, for the last picture taken at the Junior School shows me, standing on the back row, looking serious and unsure, so different from the cheeky, giggly child in her first year's class photo.

Mum would have 'home perms' buying the kits from the shops. The acrid ammonia of the perm together with the chemical that had to be applied afterwards to 'set' the perm filled the kitchen. Mum used small blue rubber curlers which had to be twisted together to keep the curl in shape. Her hair never failed to go fizzy, despite changing the timings for the lotion to be kept on. She always refused to see that there was anything the matter, "oh well it will come looser after a couple of washes."

And so my time at Oxford Road School for Girls was eventually coming to an end. I didn't think about where I was to go next. The older girls at the Maidstone Grammar School and the Technical School for Girls on our estate appeared to be very snooty in their uniforms; looking down their noses at us. We had no uniform at our school so their hats and jackets seemed very different. I didn't want to go to a school with all girls again and longed for the humour and fun that I had remembered from my mixed infant days.

As the warmer weather arrived Stephanie and I would go to the swimming baths in town on a Saturday morning. We would bus in and then save our return bus fare and walk back home across the park so that we could buy jam doughnuts after our swim. Our reddened eyes would be stinging and our skin still smelling of the chlorine that was copiously applied to the pool. By now I had managed to swim underwater. We could dive down between each other's spread-eagled legs and surface spluttering out the water. But I forgot to be careful when reaching the surface. As I gasped for air I realised that my denture plate had floated out. It was mortifying! I panicked trying to dive back down to see if I could find it but there were so many swimmers in the way that I couldn't see it.

In desperation I found one of the pimply-faced life guards, "You'll have to clear the pool!" I was almost in tears.

"No chance, you'll have to wait until the end of the session."

I couldn't go back in the water to swim but paced up and down trying to peer into the water for a glimpse of pink. It was useless. Finally the public session came to an end and the life guard dived into the water triumphantly surfacing with my plate in his hand adding to my mortification. I was wary about ever going swimming again and never dared dive into the water. My underwater swimming came to an end that day.

At school the lessons continued with the highlight being story time in the afternoon when Miss Thorgood read us stories of Heidi and her poor grandmother who yearned to have white bread rolls instead of the hard brown ones that she could barely chew. I cried when Black Beauty met poor Ginger again and was enchanted by the water babies who were afraid of the chimney sweep Tom. I wondered at his fate as he stole the tasty food from Mrs Doasyouwouldbedoneby not seeing Mrs Bedonebyasyoudid watching him from behind the rocks. Tales from the Arabian Nights and The Secret Garden caught my imagination as I eagerly awaited the next day's chapter.

Mrs Thorogood always wore a string of creamy-white pearls. At the end of one hot afternoon we sat at our desks listening to her story when suddenly the string snapped on the necklace and sent the pearls cascading over the wooden floor. We spent the rest of the afternoon trying to find all the pearls that had rolled in so many directions.

Finally the day came when the 11 Plus test papers arrived. We sat in the quiet school hall. The atmosphere was strange and disquieting. We put our names on the top of the paper and waited to start. The English papers were easy and I sailed through them but the Maths papers stumped me completely. I could do the ordinary addition, subtraction, multiplication and long division but strange sums with dots appeared. I didn't know what the dots meant. Then there were drawings of shapes with little corners with numbers inside. What did they mean? I went home quite unnerved and told Mum that I couldn't do half the sums on the paper. "Never mind I'm sure you did your best" she dismissed my fears. When Dad got home I told him. "They're decimals." I was nonplussed. We had never 'done' decimals. Now as an adult I realise that the A stream class had a set syllabus which included decimals and geometry which was not part of the B stream's remit. I didn't pass for the Grammar school. No one in my class did. We were destined for either Oldborough Manor at the back of Mangravet, Southborough Girls School down the Loose Road, which Heather had attended, or Senacre Secondary Modern School on the Sutton Road. Mum put Senacre as our first choice.

My days at Oxford Road were officially at an end.

Top: Our Aunty Sally and Marian's house in Nottingham.
Left: Me fishing in the stream at the bottom of their garden.
Right: Our tin bath and a small selection of Mum's button collection!

Below: The first year at Oxford Road Junior School (I am giggling on the 2nd row 3rd from the left). Stephanie is standing behind Miss Hunt Two more school photos when I am aged 8 and then aged 10, after I had chipped my front tooth

Top: Our Christmas fairy doll, a lead pig belonging to the farm yard, the copper kettle that refused to stay clean, a copy of Alice in Wonderland and then us at the seaside with our giant sandcastle.

My childhood treasures, including my paints, money box with old coins, Girl Guide badges, toy dog, books and Muffin the Mule.

Chapter 3   1961 – 1967 Moving on

Perhaps we did visit the new secondary school before we started in September but I can't remember any induction, or any discussion about being prepared for a new regime. In those days it was expected that you made the best of it and just got on with life. Mum had bought my new uniform from Gabriel's Hill in town. I had the navy school beret held on firmly with a couple of hair grips then there was a navy second hand blazer with the school oak leafed emblem embroidered on the front pocket. She purchased a white long-sleeved blouse, a navy and maroon tie, a navy v-necked jumper, a navy pleated skirt and finally to complete the ensemble a thick warm striped navy and maroon school scarf. Being unused to wearing a tie I felt constrained and suffocated by the uncomfortable, tightly fitting, collar around my throat. It did nothing to assuage my feelings of unease.

Sitting on the floor of the large assembly hall we waited expectantly in fidgety rows anxious to find out where we were to go. Our new satchels and school bags, holding the obligatory pencil cases, sat beside us. My stomach fluttered uncomfortably as an imposing figure sporting a head of wavy auburn hair swept past, his black gown flowing imperiously behind him. Mr Evans, our new headmaster, strode onto the stage. Other members of staff lined the walls watching us curiously from either side of the hall, whispering, their conversations hidden from us as they spoke behind their hands.

Welcoming us to his school I half-listened as his words formed meaningless sentences. It was if I was playing a part; that of a captive audience, knowing what the words meant but making no sense of his speech. My knotted stomach ensured my brain's complete incomprehension. Finally he proceeded to read out our names on his list allocating us to a nominated form teacher. Thankfully some of the pupils from my old class in Oxford Road Junior School were to still be with me but I found that I was separated from Stephanie. Gathering up our possessions we trouped to a large classroom where we spent the best part of the morning writing out a timetable of our lessons. We added detail of a single lesson or double lesson, with what teacher, and in which room the lesson would take place. A plan of the school illustrated the position of stairs, corridors and rooms. Our class was to be found upstairs overlooking the sports field. We were to keep our books and other personal effects in the desks. It was all so confusing. How we had arrived at the room was a mystery. I had no idea of how to retrace my steps or reach the outside world. We were designated a school house team. These were set up to promote healthy competition and achievement both in the classroom and on the sports field. I was pleased to be assigned the Medway house; pleased because the house was blue my favourite colour. Weald was yellow; Downs was green and Vinters was red.

The bell rang for each change of lesson; the tumultuous roar of voices and movement, the scraping of chairs on floors and numerous feet as they clattered along the corridors and down the stairs startled us. Once that hubbub had quietened our form teacher continued our instruction. Finally the bell sounded the lunch break. We were led down the stairs and into the canteen. Instead of receiving a plate of food on the table as we had had at the junior school we were instructed to line up at the serving area holding a tray. At the serving hatch we could see the huge kitchen behind those cooks standing with large spoons waiting to place the food on our plates. In later years the system was changed and we would be seated at a space at our table and be served our food from the designated 'head' of that table.

That day we discovered that we could win house points for good work and behaviour, that school prefects were there to assist the smooth running and discipline in the school, and that we needed to bring our PE kit in a bag the following day. I realised that we would be expected to go to different rooms for subject lessons but would always meet up in the form room for registration at the beginning of each day.

On the yard at break time, no longer would we refer to it as 'playtime'; we met others from our old school and those in older year groups. We were a source of curiosity and amusement in our 'oh so correct' new uniforms. I quickly learnt that the obligatory beret was never worn at the front of the head but was pushed back as far as it could go and fastened by numerous hair grips. In the girls toilets older girls backcombed their hair until the strands stood upright; the top layer of hair was smoothed over the coveted beehive, Helen Shapiro shape, and kiss curls were licked and smoothed down onto the cheek bones. Those with sticky hair lacquer sprayed their hair until a hurricane would have had difficulty in displacing the bouffant result. Thankfully they did not know that I was still wearing the obligatory long-legged navy 'drawers', as Gran would insist on calling them, and owned no brassiere despite an embarrassing slight swelling in the chest department.

Heather had stiff net petticoats in her wardrobe and it was said that you could make them even stiffer if you soaked them in a solution of dissolved sugar and let them dry naturally. Some of the older boys had imitated the Teddy Boys and had slicked hair with a carefully teased front quiff stiff with Brylcreem to keep it in place.

Outside on the yard older boys played a rough game of football, their urgent shouts alerting each other to, "Pass! Pass!"

and impatiently claiming, "Mine!"

Until finally a triumphant, "Goooooooooal!" as the scuffed heavy leather ball shot between two sets of jumpers placed on the ground.

We stood around unconsciously huddling awkwardly together for comfort watching other groups as they talked, ran boisterous 'Tag' games, or laughed at private jokes. Two prefects wandered around the yard patrolling their patch. Suddenly there were raised voices, for a moment other games and conversation died away, and then, as one, a large crowd gathered together forming a circle "Fight, Fight!" the chant began, growing in volume and excitement.

Two older lads were circling each other inside the ring. A score needed to be settled. They started to throw punches at each other. Fist met cheek with a thwack. Suddenly a teacher pushed his way through the mêlée and attempted to part the boys.

"Enough! Enough!" He grunted; trying to contain them as they squirmed away from his hold to reach each other again, their faces contorted with rage. The circle of pupils melted away as the two lads walked, half propelled towards a doorway, the teacher's hand grasping each collar securely.

We heard their protests. "He started it Sir."

"I always get the blame."

Get yer hands off me."

"I'll 'ave you later."

Their protests and appeals followed the path into school. The circle gradually dispersed.

"Now they're for it." Their plight was reviewed. "This time they'll get a suspension for sure."

"Nar it'll be expulsion."

"Bound to happen," it was confirmed.

"And how did you get on today?" Mum was there when I reached home.

"Oh fine." Where could I begin? There was too much to relate.

"I'm in the Medway House." I began.

"Oh that's nice."

"You get house points if you do good work."

"Oh," Mum sounded unsure.

"We have to take our PE kit tomorrow, and you don't have to wear a blazer, 'cos no one else does." I could see that she wasn't impressed.

"Well I haven't spent money on that for you to throw away after one day. Besides it might be cold tomorrow."

"I've got English tomorrow and then History, and Maths and then double PE." Better to change the subject than start on about the blazer.

"I'm in Form 1A now."

"Uh huh."

I took my satchel upstairs. Other children in my form had school bags. Mine bequeathed by my Aunty Betty had not only seen better days but unhappily looked so hopelessly old-fashioned compared with the navy duffle bags carelessly slung over my classmates shoulders. I hoped that soon I could dispense with the satchel and get a duffle bag too. But there were other more pressing considerations. Would I get lost in the maze of school building tomorrow; finding the right classroom for English and all the other lessons? I hoped that it would all make sense the next day.

That night I dreamt of long endless corridors, turning corner after corner, up and down stairs but never arriving at a room.

When Saturday arrived I was glad to spend the time at home. It had been a long week. Lessons were not hard and they had been surprisingly enjoyable. I had got lost trying to find the right classroom, but thankfully had been with others in my class who were equally confused so we had been rounded up sheepishly by a prefect and escorted to the right room. It was strange having to finish something, almost in mid flow, as soon as the bell sounded and then to start off again in a completely different subject. In the science room we had perched on high stools set at a long bench. Some boys in the class had been warned about turning on the Bunsen burners and filling the room with a sickly smell of gas, but a tell-tale hiss erupted from time to time from the back of the laboratory. There were large wall charts of the skeletal system and the solar system at the back of the room. We were told that we would watch experiments and then copy out notes about what we had seen. Already some in the class had been awarded house points. Their work had been returned with a large red tick and 1HP initialled in the corner, which meant that one point had been given. It was possible to have 2HP as well.

The following week I would have to miss the first period which was History as I had to go back to the Junior School to attend the foot clinic to have my verruca scraped again. They hadn't been able to cut it all out despite having the special cream and plaster applied to it.

I was a little apprehensive about being late back to school on my own. I had always been with someone else when catching the bus.

It was strangely exciting to have male teachers after the all-female environment of Oxford Juniors. Somehow they seemed more relaxed, their humour lightened any anxiety. We giggled at their jokes whilst respecting their firm control. Our stylish English teacher was called Elizabeth Thatcher. Her repertoire did not include jokes but she had no need to impress. I was captivated as soon as I saw her. Her pink-rose cheeks and peachy-cream complexion complemented a shiny bob of short black hair. And she appeared quite foreign, as if having some Italian or French ancestry in her blood. But the piercing stare over the top of her glasses reinforced a no-nonsense approach, which kept us soundly in our place. We started on simple grammar to ensure that everyone was aware of the ground rules. I had never been introduced to even the rudiments of how our language worked, but the rules, as she explained them, seemed so obvious and enjoyably simple. Verbs, adverbs, nouns, common nouns, pronouns, adjectives; she introduced them to us with memorable examples. Learning was suddenly so much fun. Our vocabulary was extended as she disdainfully dismissed the old text books that tried to tell us that 'small was the same as little', or 'funny was the same as amusing'.

"Each word has its own particular meaning", she insisted, "they may be similar but they are never the same!"

We respectfully noted her authority.

"It is for us to find out why they are different and use them appropriately. As for spellings there are rules and then there are the exceptions to the rule," she informed us.

"'I' before 'e' except after 'c' providing the sound is 'ee'," we intoned after her.

She set us titles for a composition and I was instantly flattered to be awarded a house point when she had marked the work. Her encouraging words enthused me; I was thirsty for her praise.

In the Geography class we drew maps of the British Isles and then had to mark the main towns and cities upon it in red dots. I loved the first task of having to invent a small village and use the appropriate markings and symbols to map a woodland, field, post office, church, railway, road, river and house. I got so carried away that the teacher remarked that I had created a town! But to my great satisfaction the map was awarded two house points.

After school and lunchtime clubs and societies were another feature of this progressive school. I fancied joining the choir, chess club and classical music society, although I had little understanding of musical appreciation, but Dad had taught me how to play chess and I enjoyed singing. As a family we had always played card and board games. Dad had played Cribbage, Pontoon, Contract Bridge, Whist, Patience, Gin Rummy, Canasta and Bezique. We had progressed from Happy Families, Snap, and Sevens until as a foursome we had mastered the bidding system for Contract Bridge. Every Christmas we would play Monopoly when Dad, once he had dealt out our money as the banker, would invariably manage to purchase Park Lane and Mayfair. Heather and I played Ludo and the letter game Lexicon at Gran's house.

Although we had always been told that coming from the Shepway Council Estate we would be lucky to get a job in Woolworths serving behind the counter, the atmosphere at Senacre was positive and encouraging. We were told to set our sights higher and to see what we could achieve.

A chess tournament was arranged with the Boys Grammar School. As we trouped into their red-bricked school I was conscious of the smirks of superiority on the faces of some of our opponents. I was placed towards the end of the long table as my skills were nowhere as good as some of the older, more established players in the club. Facing my opponent over the chess board, my stomach churning as I tapped one of his two proffered hands to see what colour pawn it contained. He won. Confidently his Queen's pawn stepped forward, I followed suit. His cavalry started a charge and my defensive bishops moved to aid a hapless pawn. Finally as I started to plan the following moves I could see that he expected me to take an obvious route. As I moved more pieces to block his assault a pattern of moves and counterattacks rumbled on in my head; if I move there and he takes this then I move there and offer a bishop but then the knight can come back and trap his Queen. She will be blocked ....but if he doesn't take that, then I will change the attack and move my pawn out to allow the other bishop a direct line to his King, backed by my Queen and it will be check! My thoughts rumbled on. Suddenly he fell for the trap. The bait was taken. My bishop was lost and my opponent smiled at my 'mistake'. Suddenly the way was clear on the other side of the board. He frowned at the unexpected action and moved too quickly attempting to close the attack down. He hadn't seen the pincer movement. Look both ways!

"Check."

The boy next to him glanced up hearing my announcement.

I dare not look at him in case I betrayed my next move. He breathed heavily; the clock ticked his time away. His King shuffled for safety to the side hiding behind a pawn. My knight was clear to take its bold neighbour and his King was powerless to retaliate, his retinue had fled too far to be recalled.

"Checkmate!"

Had my opponent not been so sure of himself he would have probably won, but he had made the classic mistake of underestimating the 'competition'. Firstly he judged a girl as inferior, and secondly he had assumed that coming from a secondary modern I would be a failure. I was so pleased to disappoint him.

As my horizons were widened by the teachers at Senacre so I also began to take notice of the world around me. The newspapers had never really held my attention. Now I began to appreciate that there was such a thing as a Cold War between Russia and America and that we seemed to be involved. They were also racing to conquer Space. Dogs and monkeys had first been sent up in rockets. Russian scientists and engineers were developing sputniks to whizz around the earth as they and the Americans rushed ahead to see who could reach the moon first. Then Russia sent Yuri Gagarin blasting into Space; the first manned flight. It was a sensation. We listened to the popular hit song 'Telstar' on the wireless. Now we learnt that there were to be satellites orbiting the earth and that they could be tracked from earth. Our Science Fiction stories from The Eagle were becoming fact! Then I read in the Daily Mirror that the American John Glenn had orbited the earth.

Gran fretted about the impact of the rockets and sputniks falling back to earth.

"Some of them are as big as buses!" She claimed.

"Think of the hole that they would make if they fell back. We will all be killed."

We watched the CND marches on her television as the protesters held up their circular three-pronged symbol, which appeared to me like a rocket that was to be launched.

Slowly it dawned on me that Russia had changed its name. It was now called the Soviet Union and this brought with it a renewed threat of nuclear war. I had seen pictures of the huge mushroom effect after the bombing of Hiroshima in Japan, and began to feel quite fearful of what the Super Powers would do, with us, in Britain, being the 'piggy in the middle'. The newspapers had reported something about the Bay of Pigs in Cuba and how it had been a huge political failure for the Americans and that they had not wanted to repeat that. I was confused, trying to understand why Khrushchev who was the new Soviet leader and a young, good-looking President called John F Kennedy who had replaced Eisenhower in the USA wanted to fight in Cuba again. And I wasn't even sure where Cuba was.

Slowly I realised that it seemed to be about Russian missiles and that America was also against the bearded Fidel Castro who seemed to be an outlaw or bandit of some kind. The newspaper talked of the 'continuing Communist threat' and spies. Suddenly the world didn't seem very safe at all. At home the political scandal of John Profumo hit the headlines with his affair with the dark-haired beauty Christine Keeler sitting on the wrong way on a chair, her legs alarmingly all akimbo. I didn't understand how the story fitted together. Had he sold secrets to the Russians? Was she in fact a beautiful Russian spy working alongside the other blonde spy Mandy Rice-Davies? I didn't understand the term 'call girl'. It was like a seedy James Bond film without the glamour of a dashing hero or fast car chases. Our Prime Minister the weedy, gaunt, Alex Douglas–Home was so disappointingly different from Kennedy. I began to worry if we were all going to be killed in a big nuclear war.

On Gran's television I had previously enjoyed 'What's my Line?', 'Crackerjack', and 'The Black and White Minstrel Show', now I watched CND protests and marches against the Bomb. I began to realise that adults were not infallible and it was very scary. Dad and I went along each Saturday to her house to watch the new science fiction show called Dr Who, allowing him to be cheerfully entertained, and for me to be totally scared by the robotic metallic Daleks.

About this time I decided that I wanted to join the Girl Guides. I had previously been quite scathing about the little Brownies running around in the Scout's Hut that had been built opposite our house on the other side of the road, but the idea of going on camps and having outdoor adventures rather appealed to me. I went over to the Hut one Friday night to meet the Guide Leader staying on to see 'if I liked it'. My Aunty Betty had been a Girl Guide and she still had her Guide belt and buckle so Mum only needed to buy me a blouse and skirt. After a couple of visits I was sworn in;

"I promise on my Honour to do my best, to do my duty to God and the Queen, to help other people at all times and to obey the Guide law."

I was certainly going to be 'prepared' at all times and couldn't wait to be assigned a patrol and start on the badges. There were four patrols in the group and mine was the Kingfisher patrol which pleased me as I thought that the colourful bird was the best emblem to be sewn into my uniform. I had enjoyed sewing. At the junior school I had made a gathered skirt which I had worn until it finally didn't fit. At the secondary school we started simple embroidery stitches, making small samplers to demonstrate a darn, a patch, a button hole and some hemming stitches. My neat work samples had won me praise from the needlework mistress, which gave me great satisfaction. My Gran had taught me how to knit but I had only managed a scarf that went in and out at the sides as I had lost and gained stitches on the way. We went on to learn how to make a French seam, box pleats and ordinary pleats, how to make darts and the tricky business of inserting a zip. In the needlework room there were a variety of sewing machines along one long bench. We were shown how to thread each one so that we could use any machine in a lesson.

The Domestic Science room was also a revelation. There was a self-contained kitchen area set with table and chairs and an ironing board. Various cookers, both gas and electric, were situated along one wall and preparation worktables with drawers stood in the centre of room facing the blackboard. We first had to make our own full length white apron before we could embark on any type of cookery lesson and had to make a navy pleated skirt for our PE lessons. Disappointingly our first lesson featured 'how to iron a shirt'. I discovered that the thick material at the top of the shoulders was called the yoke and that had to be ironed first, followed by the collar, cuffs, front seams, the main body of the shirt starting on the front panels, then the back before embarking on the sleeves. We copied tidy notes from the blackboard complete with illustrations about the ironing process. Next we learnt how to clean a cooker, what temperatures should be set and how to wire a three pin plug which was marginally more interesting. Still we had not handled actual ingredients and cooked anything.

Once the apron and PE skirt had been completed we finally were introduced to some metal moulds which were to shape our coconut pyramids. Triumphantly I took home my first garishly coloured red and green samples in my cookery tin but pyramids proved to be chokingly dry and almost inedible. The coarse dry desiccated coconut refused all attempts to dissolve in our saliva.

"You'll be making rock cakes next!" Dad joked.

The next week we did just that. They also went in the bin with a thud. However we then made treacle toffee. The boys in our class smelt the toffee before they saw our tins.

"Cor, just let's have a bit," they whispered to us during Mr Jones' Maths lesson about perimeters. We sneaked the sticky chunks to them but then found ourselves unable to answer any questions as our teeth became glued together. Fortunately Mr Jones had a well-developed sense of humour as we endeavoured to emancipate our teeth.

Whilst we had our cookery lessons upstairs, they had either woodwork or metal work classes in the workshops at end of the bottom corridors, so there was no reciprocal arrangement on the outcomes of the lessons. At the end of the term they did produce something on which they had practised their dove tailed joints but I'm not sure if it was a complete box or just two pieces of wood made into one.

And so we became a class that enjoyed each other's company. Friendships that endured for over forty years were forged during those first few weeks. I loved the camaraderie of a co-educational school and the enthusiasm of the teachers as they set us challenges and projects. The interest that I had had at the infant school that had been so subdued at the junior school all came back to me. I was excited and my interest was noted.

Meanwhile after a short while with the Guides I was excited to find that a 'camp' had been arranged for the Easter break and that I was allowed to go.

Mum sorted through the list of requirements for the trip:

Groundsheet
Sleeping bag
Sheet for inside the sleeping bag
Pyjamas
Underwear (two sets)
Penknife
Camp Uniform (shorts and tee-shirt)
Boots
Metal food tray, mug, knife, fork, spoon
Wash bag and small towel

And so the list went on. At last I was going to experience a Swallows and Amazons Adventure!

But there were some problems; Mum could not afford a Guide tee-shirt or a pair of regulation navy shorts. I had an old blue sleeveless top that she decided would do and a friend had given her a pair of black and white shorts that just about fitted me. She set about dying the shorts navy blue. When they were dry we could still see the strips of dark and a lighter blue, but she insisted that they would have to do if I wanted to go on the trip. I was mortified. I had already gained some height, developed a bust which embarrassed me, and now I would look quite different wearing the seriously obvious striped shorts. How you long to be the same when you are young! Still there was no help for it.

We arrived in a field and were detailed to erect our tent. We strained to position guy ropes and to bang pegs into the unforgiving ground. Eventually the tent was up. Positioning our groundsheets around the tent we piled our belongings on top before going out to sit in a Guide Circle to receive the first set of instructions.

We learnt that the canvas was on no account to be touched when it was raining as this would interfere with the wet-proofing and cause drips inside. Then we were to construct some 'gadgets' using the sticks and string provided to construct a support for a washing up bowl; a rack for the dishes and utensils, and a larger rack to place our clothes away from the ground so that they would not get damp. Points for each tent would be awarded according to the best construction. Within the camps there general jobs; first a 'latrine duty', which involved digging a latrine hole then erecting a small tent around it, and a 'cooks duty' which involved helping to prepare breakfast, the evening meal and washing and scouring the large pots and pans. Thankfully I managed to avoid latrines, did a minimum amount of pot scrubbing, managed to avoid the rain spots during the night and constructed a 'gadget' that didn't collapse when a washing bowl was set upon it. Although it was my first night away from home and my 'homesickness' surprised me it didn't overshadow the first experience of camping out under canvas.

Meanwhile Heather had a Saturday job working at Chieseman's and was at college during the week, having successfully applied for the Commercial Art course at the Maidstone College of Art, so I saw less of her; although there were times when she was left in charge of me

119

on the rare occasions when Mum and Dad went to a Parent's evening.

"Now that they are out you are to do as I say."

Her imperious tone enraged me.

"No I don't !"

We continued to clash as our personalities took us in different directions. Her air of superiority maddened me. We argued and fought, banging doors and shrieking at each other. One day I was brought to such a pitch that I lost control threatening to 'kill her' as I raced up the stairs. She locked herself in the bathroom and left me outside unable to get at her. I kicked at the door pulling and twisting the unrelenting handle.

"Open this door! Wait 'till I get you!" I could just imagine her self-satisfied, smug look knowing that she was safe inside."

Dad had to drag me away still convulsed with fury. Goodness how that particular row had started but my assault on the hapless bathroom door passed down into family folklore. As did the time when I had stupidly locked the bathroom door and then couldn't release the lock mechanism. Dad had to borrow a ladder and squeeze in though the small window to release a very tearful and contrite child.

During my first couple of years at Senacre we still experienced thick smogs during the winter months. I can remember having to feel my way home touching the small garden walls for guidance, stepping off unexpected kerbs with a jolt and finding a street lamp temporarily lighting the route before being plunged into the grey–green swirl of fog again. But the winter of 1963 provided us with the most severe weather starting in the December 1962 and continuing until the end of February 1963. My bedroom became so cold that Mum decided that I would have to share with Heather. The windows retained a thick leaf pattern; the sill collected a pool of frozen water whilst under the window the walls were streaked and bubbled with traces of water and condensation. Mum had purchased a pink elliptical electrical heater that could be placed inside the bed to warm it up and get rid of the dampness, but the extreme cold rendered it almost useless. As the snow fell steadily gardens, paths, trees and bushes and houses were enveloped in a soft white bulky blanket. We awoke to an unnatural silence. No cars came round the bend in our road; it was as if the world had stopped. Ice and frost formed on each new layer of snow until the thick crust was able to support us. We tramped across to the park, our wellington boots sometimes suddenly sinking down through the frozen crust until we were stuck in two to three feet of snow. The lake was frozen solid with a thick sheet of ice so thick that those that were bold enough could walk right across it. We still walked to school revelling in the new landscape of the familiar route; dodging snowball fights and friendly ambushes on the way. There was a code of honour in these fights. No ice to be packed in the snowball and no aiming for the head. Most fights obeyed the code but inter-school rivalry could present some dangers and were best avoided. Take the storm of snowballs, don't retaliate and get past fast!

The snow lasted for weeks and weeks until finally it turned into grey slush. We had had enough of it by then. The novelty had worn off and the inconvenience of constant damp washing hanging over the wooden clothes horse in the dining room or around the fire in the front room pervading the house with a stale musky smell exasperated Mum and us all.

Dad had always enjoyed the cinema and by 1962 he had taken both Heather and I to see the James Bond films at the Granada in Maidstone at the bottom of Gabriel's Hill. We saw Dr No, Russia with Love and later Goldfinger there, sometimes coming in halfway through the B film and sitting there until it was back to where we had started. If we happened on the last performance we would race to see if we could get out of the auditorium before the playing of the National Anthem. As luck would have it some people at the end of the aisle were infuriatingly slow. And so we reluctantly stood to attention until the last strains of the tune on a stretched tape came to an end.

With a friend I joined a long queue that snaked up King Street, along the alleyway leading to the River Len before finally reaching the Ritz Cinema to see Cliff Richard in Summer Holiday. Immersed in the picture I desperately wanted to be Sandy and join him on the bus. I was beginning to feel quite grown up. We even went into the milk bar in Gabriel's Hill next to the old Palace Theatre and had a coffee perched on a high stool feeling very sophisticated. Previously the Pathe News introduced by the shrill rooster had bored me before until I finally began to realise that the described events had something to do with my own life. Suddenly I saw hoards of screaming girls calling for John Paul, Ringo and George as the 'fab four' descended the aircraft steps. But it was on the wireless on the Friday after a Girl Guide meeting on 22nd November 1963 that I heard the shocking report of the assignation of John F Kennedy. It has always been said that most people remember where they were on that occasion. For me it was the first time that I realised that events and circumstances could alter our entire way of life. I was shocked by the revelation, having in my naivety believed that people in public life were immune to assaults and tragedies. It was as if the 'good guy' in the white Stetson had been gunned down by the 'baddie'. It couldn't happen. Just wind back the film; there is a mistake in the plot. I knew the format; he said a fond farewell to the 'gal' back home and rode out into the sunset to right the wrongs of another day. But this happening to a President that was young and good looking wasn't right. I was chilled by it and frightened for the future; the cold war, and all the directions about preparing for a nuclear war that we were given at school. 'If you are outside in a field find a suitable dip and lie down; if at home make sure that you fill the bath with water, whitewash the windows and place tape in a criss-cross design across each panel, stock up with tinned and packet food and clear an area under the stairs for an improvised shelter. Do no look directly at the blast, but turn away from the light.' We were shown the booklet 'Advising the Householder on protection against Nuclear Attack', and now we were told that there were plots to assassinate the great and the good.

The newspaper screamed about the Great Train Robbery reporting that an amazing two million pounds had been stolen. We couldn't begin to imagine such an enormous amount of money. It was audacious. Dad dryly commented that at least Beeching hadn't managed to close that train line down. I became vaguely aware that an American black man called Luther King had made an important 'I

Have a Dream' speech' but it wasn't until I read about the black girls being massacred in a church in Alabama that I connected this speech with what was happening to the black people in America. I had only had one immediate connection with a black girl in my class in the junior school. I saw no black people in our local town or had thought about their position in the deep southern states of America. I knew that there were black jazz musicians and film stars but they existed in another world. I was frightened by the violent images of riot police and dogs holding back demonstrators. People seemed to be so angry and out of control.

My nightmares took on new directions. Helicopters and spy planes would circle around our house. At first it was just a small group of planes flying over searching for something but then they came back. They had been listening in to our conversation and we had said something wrong. They could hear though windows and walls. There was no escape as the helicopter hovered just outside the window, shining their light into the room. And down in the garden a small pond of goldfish was seething. As I watched there seemed to be bigger and bigger fish, writhing together, using up all the space and water, giant eels writhing and gasping for air, thrashing their tails, filling the garden with a sea of monstrous eels in grey thickening mud. No way out of the house. Goggled men, breathing through thick tubes coming silently through the windows, eels oozing through the mud below, I was trapped by them all......................

Along Willington Street towards the Ashford Road were the strawberry fields. Heather and I would sometimes go in June to earn some extra pocket money. Each picker was given a tray containing twenty-four punnet boxes, and shown which line to pick. It was back breaking stuff. We had strict instructions not to pick unripe, or damaged fruit; not to 'plug' the fruit but to twist the strawberry from the stalk so that the green frill and stalk were still attached. Each punnet needed to be filled to the brim and if they were underweight when we went to the weighing machine or had included bruised or plugged fruit then we would not be paid for the whole tray. For each filled tray we would receive 2/6d.If we picked well we could earn ten shillings in one day. To pick a whole tray and then not to be paid was something that we had witnessed, having seen other inexperienced pickers have their trays rejected. There was no argument to be made. As the fruit had to travel up to the London markets in prime condition the farmer ensured that he would not risk his livelihood and his profit by losing to our carelessness.

He did allow us to eat some fruit whilst picking as long as we kept up a steady supply of filled trays and at the end of the afternoon we could fill a small basket to take home at a reduced rate. Most of the pickers were seasoned strawberry-stained, black-fingered, travelling Gypsies who went from farm to farm during the year. Some picked hops in the autumn and others potatoes, apples, pears, raspberries and cherries as they travelled through the farms in Kent. Their tanned faces recorded an outdoor life and they watched to see how painfully slow we were against them. Weighing in three or four trays to one of ours they never had their trays refused. When 'hopping' they slept in the huts in the fields joined by some East Enders from London who came down annually with their whole family to work in the fields. The children watched the prowess of the older family members as the delicate frilly-leaved hops were stripped from the long branches by hand, put into huge bins to be tallied before being taken in sacks to the oast houses for drying.

We loved taking the bus and winding down through the villages of Marden and Goudhurst before reaching Cranbrook with Mum and Dad, passing the apple and cherry orchids full of pink and white blossom in the spring and laden with heavy fruit in the autumn. I marvelled at how quickly the hops managed to reach the top of the poles before heavily trailing along the ropes mingling together in a profusion of tangled green.

Dad appreciated the beauty of the countryside, of gardens and landscapes but had long since given up harvesting his crops at home. The novelty of the early years had worn thin. He became frustrated by the weeds and bindweed that strangled the plants and the constant battle against bugs that fed on them. As I asked for more of our garden to dig, so he was happy to concede. Eventually I turned the entire back garden planting my own vegetables and fruit. I made bonfires of the weeds and turned the ashes back into the ground. One day I pulled at a particularly reluctant dandelion and found something glinting embedded in its root. It turned out to be Dad's signet ring that he had lost years before. Dad couldn't wear it as it had been bent and twisted by the root structure of the weed but he was pleased as punch that I had unearthed it.

"Well I never expected to see that again!"

By now he acquired some indoor pleasures having the use of a new record player and purchased some steam train records which we were supposed to enjoy with him.

"Listen to the slippage as she comes down that bend!"

We nodded or shook our heads at the appropriate time but had no idea what he was talking about, nor had the faintest interest to find out.

Next he started to take an interest in embroidery, designing magnificent Chinese dragons using gold thread, brilliant beads and sparking sequins on a background of black or deep blue velvet, buying his specialist threads and beads from the large department store, Ricemans, in Canterbury. Then he turned his hands to weaving; making tartan style scarves for each member of the family with uncomfortable, scratchy, wool, but we wore them never the less in honour of his skill. He set about making a Mah Jong set complete with four little box trays for the 'tiles' and a box to contain the whole set. Each tile was carefully scribed and coloured with inks. I loved handling the dragons and winds, the flowers and seasons. But before we built the Great Wall of China with the tiles they had to be shuffled: 'the twittering of the sparrows' ensued.

As he now had a 'gammy' leg he decided to purchase a car. His choice was a 'Racing Green' Bond as it was the cheapest that he could afford and being a three wheeled car with no reverse gear he did not have to take driving test. It had two seats at the front and a tiny shelf type seat at the back. One late afternoon he decided to take us to see the re-released Walt Disney film, Fantasia, which was showing at Tenterden. On the way home the Bond developed some mysterious but catastrophic mechanical failure so Heather was told to sit in the front and steer whilst Dad and I pushed the car. Unfortunately we had managed to reach the steep hill at Sutton Valence before the car died. It was a very, very, long journey home, not helped by the fact that Heather, being a novice at the wheel, kept driving into the kerb, much to Dad's frustration.

By this time I had had enough of the Girl Guide Movement. I had expected 'Great Adventures' but we spent our time playing games, collecting things and attending various church parades, which bored me. I decided to leave them to it.

Heather repeated family history by taking a summer job at Sharps Toffee factory that summer in order to earn a bit more money. The Saturday job at Chiesemans hardly paid for her bus fare to college during the week and she wanted to save up for a holiday abroad. The year before she had booked a holiday to Greece but had omitted to tell Mum first. Mum went ballistic and stormed down to the travel agent to cancel it. She was afraid that Heather was not old enough at seventeen to go on holiday alone. Heather was furious that her plans had been thwarted.

"When I'm eighteen next year you can't stop me!" and the rows raged on.

I began to realise that we were not the only family to suffer quarrels. As I lay in bed on a quiet Sunday morning, our visits to the Baptist church at an end, I could hear the neighbours across the road shouting at each other. The routine began. I heard her voice, being higher and shriller loud and clear, but occasionally her husband's low responses also carried in the air. The usual conclusion was for him to come storming out of the front door and stride down the lane towards the park telling her that she could,

"F..... off!"

Her screams followed him, reminding him not to come back, prompting him to tell her that he had no intention of doing so.

Next door the two sisters quarrelled and doors regularly banged to make their point more obvious.

"Oh dear they're at it again," Mum shook her head.

Down the road we knew that one of the husbands regularly beat up his thin silent wife. He was a huge stocky man, and I was quite afraid of him whenever he passed by, making sure that I never met his eye.

I lay listening to the noises of the estate, dogs barking, banging of doors, Mum and Dad arguing, she, about his poor wages, and him, why his packed lunch wasn't ready when she knew that he was going out, wishing that I could be somewhere else.

I continued to escape into books. At Senacre a new 'library' cupboard had been made available to us stocking paperbacks so I eagerly started to explore a different kind of literature in its novel format. But first I used the school's main library exhausting their selection of 2nd World War books reading 'Carve her name with Pride', 'Anne Franks Diary' and other stories of espionage and spies. It was a peculiar passion probably prompted by the 1961 film 'Guns of Navarone' and from feeding on a diet of films that had been made in the 1950's, 'The Dam Busters', 'Reach for the Sky', 'The Cruel Sea' and 'Ice Cold in Alex'. I worried about how I would have survived interrogation, about being brave and how another war could start again. By this time I also knew that I did not believe in a God. I had decided that if there was truly, no beginning or end, then logically there couldn't be a God since that signified a beginning. With my diet of science fiction I felt that there had to be an infinite number of universes all containing different planets and some worlds much like our own. And I also reasoned that loving, caring, Christian God could not deliberately create such dreadful mayhem; from fires, earthquakes, floods and pestilence or condone horrendous wars and terrible individual acts of violence and suffering. And if there was a God who did indeed set out to cause so much torment and misery then why would I want to worship such a cruel deity. Our school day began with an assembly but I could no longer join in with the Lord's Prayer. I felt outside a faith but I couldn't be hypocritical.

The paperback library meanwhile held numerous treasures. First there was 'The Greengage Summer', 'Catcher in the Rye', 'Cider with Rosie', 'Billy Liar', 'Room at the Top', 'The Loneliness of the Long

Distance Runner', 'The Prime of Miss Jean Brodie', the 'Darling Buds of May'; the contemporary books had been carefully selected and I devoured them greedily.

The days at school flew by. I found the lessons so interesting and the teachers encouraging. There was a sense of 'us against the common perception of the ordinary secondary modern school kid' at the school, and there was good humour. We enjoyed each others company. I had already made many friends in the class and started to appreciate the different nature and qualities of the individuals within it. I was no longer in awe of the grown up prefects who had appeared to be middle-aged, just like members of staff, when I first started. I joined the choir, started to become more proficient on the hockey field and became aware that the teachers enjoyed taking our class. They spoke about us in warm tones as if we were unique and so we became what we felt they saw in us. We had a class identity. As each teacher encouraged our development so we paid them back in our respect and self regulated those who would seek to disrupt a lesson. I stayed on after school for hockey or choir practice or went to a chess tournament. I went round to my friend Pat's to have tea with her. Her Mum gave them sandwich spread on sliced bread. We never bought sandwich spread and Mum only ever bought whole loaves that needed be sliced at home. I was seriously impressed.

At home we listened avidly to Alan Freeman's Pick of the Pops on the wireless, as he welcomed us to his show each week, 'Hi there Pop Pickers', impatiently waiting to find which single had made it to number 1 in the Hit Parade. We sang along to the Beatles 'From Me to You', 'Please Please Me', and 'She Loves You', as they kept tightly hold of their prime position. Sometimes Gerry and the Pacemakers would get a look in with 'You'll Never Walk Alone' or we accompanied Helen Shapiro when she went 'Walking back to happiness'. I never did like Elvis Presley or Petula Clark and was pleased when the Beatles regained their number one spot with 'I Want to hold Your hand'. We were lyric perfect with all the latest chart stoppers singing on the way to school or devising impromptu concerts on the school yard, able to imitate each performer with their individual style and backup arrangements. We could ooh and ahhh with the best of them.

It was announced at school that there would be a set of exams for entry to the Technical boys and separate Technical Girls schools who took children aged thirteen. I was horrified by the prospect of leaving the school and attending a girl's school. I had hated my time at the junior school and didn't want to be embroiled in the spiteful cliques that girls were so good at devising. But what to do? I didn't want to fail another set of exams. My pride would be hurt and I would be letting down Mum and Dad. I agonised over the dilemma. Perhaps I would find the exams too hard and fail anyway. I fretted over it. Could I cope with knowing that some girls in my own street might pass and would look down on me, just as those did who had passed for the 11 plus? It would confirm those who had not seen fit to pass me when I was eleven. I worried at the problem but could not see an answer.

The exam arrived. We sat in the large school hall, put our names on the paper and waited to begin. The first set of papers included English grammar and a composition piece. The exam was to be in two parts. A second part would follow later.

I waited impatiently, desperate to show off my ability but frightened to accept the consequences. We were given the results. I had passed the first part. Walking home that afternoon my head buzzed. 'You have to try to pass. But I don't want to go!' Just try and see what happens, but Mum would never let me turn it down. If I passed I would have to 'go'. Round and round the voices kept arguing. That night I lay awake. Would I always be shown up as a failure if I didn't pass? As I closed my eyes I could see the girls in their neat yellow and grey uniform and their prissy hats looking down their noses at us in ours. Now I knew what to do. I had to fail. I couldn't leave a school that made me so happy. But I could never tell Mum and Dad what I had done. It would have to remain a secret and I would have to live with the prospect of 'second time' failure.' 'Mmm she wasn't even able to get into the Tech school.' I could hear the sneers; the humiliation hurt, and my chest became tight. I felt tears of self pity dampening my pillow. I don't want that! I could hear Mum talking. 'Oh yes, her daughter went to the grammar school, she was so clever.' And by implication I hadn't and wasn't!

When we were seated for the second set of exams I mechanically wrote my name in the space at the top and waited for the instructions. My pulse seemed to be thumping in my neck. Thump, bump, thump, bump.

Someone coughed, a seat scraped back, papers rustled; I looked up at the clock, the exam began.

I didn't pass for the Maidstone Technical School for Girls aged thirteen.

Then there was the pop scene, despite my absorption of the 1960's pop scene we still had no television, vaccum cleaner, refrigerator or fitted carpets at home. Mum still pushed the carpet sweeper over the carpet square, and the milk went sour in the summer. Heather had started to make her own clothes for college and so I began; starting with easy patterns, first choosing dresses that had no awkward sleeves to set in. Fortunately the 'shift' style dress was in fashion and so I was able to pin a simple paper pattern onto a relatively small amount of material. The first cut was always difficult. Would I make a terrible mistake and waste my precious length of material? My heart was in my mouth until I had completely pinned and cut round all the parts. It was also touch and go whether the zip would stay nicely hidden with the edges meeting neatly together.

The rows about money escalated. Heather was told that perhaps she would be better off getting a full time job but Dad was adamant that she would stay and complete her Diploma at college. One evening Heather brought home an exotic creature; her Egyptian friend Despina, who was on the same course as her. Despina had beautiful large almond shaped brown eyes, long elegant limbs and flawless olive skin; her clothes seem to float around her. I was captivated. Dad was pleased to be able to show off his Arabic, which she actually responded to, praising his pronunciation. I was proud on his behalf. Suddenly Heather's life style seemed so enviably different and special. I longed to have something special in my life.

Mum had taken on a different domestic job with another family in Willington Street and had enough money to buy a spin dryer. So in the kitchen we still had the old coke boiler for hot water, a slightly newer washing machine with an automatic wringer and the new spin dryer. Unfortunately the washing machine still needed to be dragged out into the centre of the room and filled using a pipe attached to the sink tap and once the washing had been rinsed and squeezed we loaded it into the spin dryer which then took on a life of its own as circled its way across the floor.

"Hold on to it!"

Our job was to half-sit on it as it built up to a full spin, trying to prevent it from careering into the cupboards.

By the age of thirteen I had lost much of the earlier puppy fat and had acquired a new hair style with a fringe. We liked to wear our jumpers long and baggy and then hitch up our skirts above the regulation length. I still had long white socks, although some other girls were wearing nylons; but generally there was no individual style to be had. We complained about having to aware a uniform, loudly protested our individuality by copying the latest fashion trend, and all ended up looking exactly the same.

Then it was announced; an end of school dance! I was devastated. What could I wear? I had no dress at all. My latest school skirt was a straight grey one in place of the very old pleated one that I had grown out of and I had a black and red shiny blouse that was fairly new. I was mortified. I would have to wear them; something new was out of the question. Heather volunteered to do something with my hair. I used to put up her hair into a French pleat every morning using copious amounts of hair grips. Her long plaits had been cut off years before. Although my hair was shorter than hers it could, perhaps, be swept up into a curly top bun, looking a bit like Shirley Bassey did in the newspapers.

I sat in the dining room, knowing that everyone would know that the grey skirt was my school skirt and that the blouse did not match it at all. I was to wear American Tan stockings held up by an uncomfortable suspender belt with fiddly rubber buttons. Heather started inexpertly pinning the curls around the base of the top bun. When she had finished I went upstairs to look in the mirror. It felt a little insecure but it would have to do. Walking up to school that evening I could feel that wind tugging at the hair grips and undoing the curls. By the time I arrived in the school foyer I knew that it had all worked loose. I went to toilets and took down the remaining mess. Towards the end of the evening, after watching the older pupils expertly jiving and doing the 'twist' to the Beatles 'Twist and Shout', I was finally was asked for a 'smooch' by a boy in the year above me with serious halitosis. The dance was not a success.

In the new term we had a different English teacher. A young handsome John Hipkin joined the staff. He provoked discussion and debate and it was a tactic that fazed me for a while. I was unsure about the idea of challenging figures of authority. It was a strange concept. He introduced topics, some bizarre and others quite emotive. Fox hunting; is it cruel or should it be considered a sport? As he read Reynard the fox to us I could feel myself caught up in the horror of the hunted animal frantically running to ground only to find his den earthed over as the hounds got closer threatening to tear him apart. The next lesson he posed a question, 'what's in a name? We were bewildered by what he meant.

"And you Julia Payne. Perhaps a descendant of that famous radical man named Thomas Paine"

I was completely ignorant of this person; totally out of my depth but particularly proud to share my name with someone in the distant past whom he obviously thought was so important. Others in the class were identified but I didn't listen I was lost in the reverie of my own, hugging the knowledge that had made me special for a few moments. I was puffed up by a sense of unexpected but utterly beguiling superiority.

At the beginning of some lessons he would share a particularly good piece of written work by other members of the class with us all. We had previously had individual pieces of work returned, marked, annotated, corrected, awarded house points but never known public acclaim. It was exciting. We were being coaxed into understanding the power of the written word, beginning to recognise each other's worth. We could share in the success of a fellow pupil. It was so novel, so different. We were as one, learning from each other. His introduction to poetry was fresh and exciting, funny, emotional unlike any poetry that I had encountered before. And it was relevant. We looked at stories in the newspapers; talked about the impact of the headlines. What was behind the story? Why did the reporter want to write it in that way? Were there two sides to the story in the article? Was it 'the truth, the whole truth, and nothing but the truth?' We were shown two different newspapers reporting the same story. Why were they different? Are we being asked to agree or disagree? My mind was sometimes left reeling by the intensity of the ideas that questioned how we viewed ourselves and the world around us. I had always taken so much of the news at face value. There was a faint glimmer of recognition when he said "the pen is mightier than the sword."

He told us about a new film that had been released. "It is called 'Lord of the Flies'." We didn't know any thing about it, having never heard of the author William Golding.

"Although the film has an X certificate rating I think that you are mature enough to see it," he said.

We went together as a group. My heart pounded with fear as the ragged boys hunted their bespectacled quarry. The film haunted me. I had understood the message about the veneer of civilisation too well; of society breaking down, and it frightened me. It was my first taste of Armageddon aged thirteen.

The following year our parents were informed that there was to be a school trip abroad. We had the opportunity of going to Switzerland. Mum and Dad discussed it and finally decided that they would draw out the Prudential Insurance. The account would be closed and they would have the thirty pounds to pay for it. I was aware that I needed to have things to wear. Apart from my school uniform I had little in the way of a 'wardrobe' of clothes. Thankfully the shift dress style was still in vogue. Mum and I went to Loder and Paynes in Bank Street to find some material. In the end I made three dresses cut from the same pattern. Girls still did not wear trousers. I didn't know anyone except for my Aunt Sally that did wear 'slacks' although women wore them in the films. The trip started in the school car park and we excitedly found our seat on the coach.

Previously I had had a day trip to Calais with the school. I had come back with two dolls wearing national costume, one for Heather and one for me. One of the boys had tried to bring back a penknife and it had been confiscated by a teacher. We had walked around the town, looked in some shops, had a paddle on the beach, and brought our souvenirs before catching the ferry sailing home.

This was to be a different adventure. We had the itinerary. We were to stay in a hotel in Kandersteg, visit a cheese factory, go to the zoo in Bern, see how cuckoo clocks and other wooden products were made and explore the mountainous locality. I was allowed to take Mum's camera to record the holiday. We did climb a mountain or were taken to the top by cable car but when we reached the summit it was covered in a thick mist. Cows wearing large bells around their necks loomed out of the grey swirling clouds and retreated again the sound of the bells clanging as they went. I was delighted with the hotel. The chalet-style wooden building was decorated and festooned with flowering hanging baskets on the balconies and they had placed large boulders of stone on the roof. At the back of the hotel in the fields grazed a herd of cows, wearing different sized bells which tinkled in different tones as they moved around. It was quite magical. We girls shared one large dormitory style bedroom and the boys were allocated a dormitory well away from us, with teachers occupying the rooms in between to ensure no nocturnal fraternisation took place. Our meals were taken in the large dining room. Waitresses wore their traditional costume covered with large white aprons constantly enquiring if we required 'cheeps more cheeps?'

I bought my souvenirs back for the family; a decorated wooden bowl for Mum, a long tasselled pipe for Dad and a doll in national costume for Heather and sending postcards to all the members of our family saying what a lovely time we were having. The PE teacher Miss Oldershaw took us for a row across the lake, we went to a concert and revelled in the pretty towns and beautiful countryside, but all too soon the coach came to start the long journey home.

At home the country seemed to be beset with a different kind of trouble. A mass of marauding Mods and helmeted Rockers roared into the seaside towns on their scooters and bikes looking for trouble. The Daily Mirror headlined their fights as they swung chains and anything else that they could use as a weapon at each other, 'Scooter gangs beat up Clacton', 'Wild Ones invade seaside- 97 arrests'. We were appalled. And it seemed contagious as each new Bank Holiday or weekend approached so swarms of bikers seemed to assemble in the next designated war zone. First Clacton was targeted and then Brighton hosted a battle.

"What is the world coming to!" the frightened older residents were scandalised.

"They should bring back National Service."

The National Service had been disbanded in 1960 much to the disgust of most of the older generation who had either served in the war or undertaken their duty in the post war service.

"It would never have happened in our day."

"I blame that Harold Wilson. He's a communist if ever there was one, a real Red under the bed."

Yet it was the same people who had said that they wanted to be rid of the Tory rule and that 'awful' Macmillan. Dad was pleased to have a new labour government. He identified with the party and their links with the unions, having witnessed the depression of 1936 and was proud to be called working class. And yet, confusingly, at work he still seemed to happily accept his poor working conditions and a wage that kept his family without the comfort that his neighbours enjoyed. He never pressed for a wage rise or complained when summoned to work in the middle of the night to deal with an emergency. He took no payment, returned home and then still turned in the next morning. He spoke quite deferentially about his boss Major Pitt and would not countenance any criticism of how the mill was being run although it was obvious, even at that time, how badly the company was doing; trying to compete with better equipped companies and more modern machinery. There was only so much that Dad could do to coax the antiquated steam driven engines into life. Even making bits and pieces for the machines on his own lathe at home, time would eventually claim its victims.

We knew that we were not as poor as another family in the street whose father had been unemployed for years, suffering from poor mental health. When we were younger we had been told that he suffered from 'shell shock'. His timid, thin, careworn wife had come to see Mum,

"Could you lend me 2/6d Mrs Payne; I'll pay you back at the end of the week?"

And Mum knew that she would pay it back; that the loan would nag and worry at her until the debt had been cleared and the slate wiped clean, so that she would be able to ask again if circumstances demanded it.

By now the fashion of the day dictated that we wore thick black diamond-patterned tights beneath our hitched up skirts and elongated sloppy jumpers. The desired effect included Rimmel pale lipstick, pan-stick makeup and lashings of mascara. The school took exception to the lipstick and mascara but we managed to trowel on the pan-stick foundation cream, which hid most of the pimples and squeezed blackheads that always threatened to emerge at the most inappropriate time. Every morning I checked in the mirror to find if another eruption had taken place during the night. A slightly raised pimple was a calamity, a personal affront to my wellbeing. Just as excruciating period pains that refused to be quelled despite an aspirin and a hot water bottle so I found no solace in Mum's reassurances that the spot 'didn't show'. I knew it showed. It stood out like a beacon! I would be mortified. Happily my fringe could cover those on the forehead, but for a pimple on the chin, traitorously throbbing and threatening to grow, a thick coating of pan-stick foundation was the only option.

And although we believed ourselves to be so grown up we still lingered by the children's playground on the way home and set ourselves on the swings after consuming the battered 'scratchings' that we had bought from the fish and chip shop on Northumberland Avenue.

I still had very little confidence outside the security of the classroom, despite being in the school choir, and only took very minor parts in any school production. My part in Bernard Shaw's Pygmalion was as the 'sarcastic bystander', a part that apparently fitted me perfectly according to one of the newer members of the English staff.

Elizabeth Thatcher introduced us to 'choral speaking'. We learnt by rote two poems for an end of term school performance, snatches that I recall even now

'Do you remember an Inn, Miranda,
do you remember an Inn…
And the tedding and the spreading
Of the straw for a bedding
and the fleas that tease in the high Pyrenees
and the wine that tasted like tar?'

"Is anyone there?' said the Traveller,
 Knocking on the moonlight door.
And his horse, in the silence, champ'd the grasses
Of the forest's ferny floor.'

I think it was Grahame who was given the task of reciting 'Osymandus, a poem written in the grand classic style that made very little sense to me then. But the language thrilled me. The eloquence, alliteration and onomatopoeic words caught at my senses, even if the sentiments escaped me.

After a hockey practice at the end of school Miss Oldershaw took me to one side.
"What career have you in mind when you leave school Julia?"
"I want to be a hairdresser."
She shook her head.

"Don't put yourself down; I've heard from the other staff that you are doing very well. You could go to college you know".

I was both flattered and yet frightened. I had not seriously considered a career. Mum had said that she wanted me to be a librarian, 'as you always have your head stuck in a book; it's a very respectable job'. But college, what would I do at college? I didn't want to work in an office and take the secretarial course that girls were offered in the 4th year.

"We have some years which are good years for students." She went on. I had no idea what she was talking about.

"Your year happened to be a very good one. Most of the students here in your class, in any other year would not be with us, they should have been in the Grammar school, you included."

"But I failed the 11 plus." I was confused.

"Every year there can only be a certain amount of children that can go to the Grammar. There are only so many places. If there is a glut of good students, the Grammar can still only take their quota."

It was the first time that I was aware of such a thing. Then I wasn't a failure after all!

"We think that your class is exceptional"

Exceptional! What a wonderful word! My world was overflowing.

The next day I caught her eye across the dining hall and smiled but she walked towards me frowning and lifting my chin and turning the collar of my blouse she announced.

"You need to go home at once!"

I was stunned.

"German Measles!"

My mortification was turned to relief; I was only ill, thank goodness for that! I thought that I had done something wrong.

I had the rest of the week off.

Towards the end of that year we were looking at subjects that we could take for our O 'level's in the 5th form. A new exam for Secondary schools was to be brought in and were to be run alongside the O 'levels to validate their levels. It was to be the CSE –Certificate of Secondary Education. We could not take A 'Levels at our school.

It was decided that as a class they would run the two syllabuses together so we would take three subjects at 'O' level, which were: English Language, Household Cookery and Mathematics. Then we would take a further six subjects at CSE level being: Art & Crafts, English, Housecraft-Cook & Hostess, Mathematics, Science of Living and Social Economics.

But before that Dad, Mum and I were going to spend a week up in Wales with his sister Sally. She had started a new job as Matron at a large mental hospital in Denbigh and we had been invited to stay there with her. Previously we had enjoyed our family visits to Nottingham staying with Marion and Tadek but this time Heather would not be accompanying us.

We took the train from Maidstone, via Euston, on to Chester, passing through the now closed station of Mold and on to Denbigh where Sally met us in her green Morris Minor estate.

I was captivated by the imposing Victorian stone built hospital and the modern white building, built specially for the nurses, all contained in neat cultivated grounds. There were numerous outbuildings, and an impressive set of wrought iron gates that fronted the long drive. We had been allocated two bedrooms and took breakfast with her in her own matron's quarters. The silver trays were laden with delights of a cooked breakfast after we had feasted on grapefruit segments, and cereals. A magnificent silver tea set was set upon the sideboard, from which she took the teapot and poured out cups of strong tea. I grandly used the silver sugar tongs to plop in a few lumps of glistening white lumps of sugar into the fine white china cup trimmed with a lace trail of gold.

Our itinerary was placed before us. There was to be a trip to Liverpool, a visit to the International Eisteddfod in Llangollen and a look round Denbigh Castle. She had allowed time out of her busy schedule to drive us down the Conway Valley past Bodnant Gardens and then on to Betws y Coed, a quick walk up to Fairy Glen and then on to Swallow Falls, the Ugly House before reaching Caernarfon Castle. An overnight stay in her caravan at Abersoch was also planned for later on that week, time permitting. As usual Time had to

139

do her bidding. It, like us, had very little choice. The week flew by. It rained in Liverpool; we spent ages waiting for her each morning before setting off at a furious pace through the narrow roads of Denbigh town. And then, frustratingly, at each stopping off point she would engage the local tradesmen in long conversations whilst we kicked our heels. The car would be piled high with her purchases, Welsh woollen blankets, local pottery bowls and wine goblets, leather handbags, Mead made by monks from a monastery, honey and preserves and anything else that took her fancy. For the trip to Whistling Sands and then down to her caravan, a large wicker hamper contained provisions for the duration of our stay.

Our homecoming was an austere anti-climax after the bountiful days spent with her.

Then back at school we discovered that we were to have a new addition to our class. A boy had been expelled from the Grammar School and as the Local Education Authority had an obligation to place him at a school, Senacre, our Secondary Modern School, was chosen to accommodate him. He swaggered into the class and threw himself onto a chair, letting it tilt back on two legs as he ran his hand through his thick black tousled hair. His dark eyes flashed a warning, 'don't mess with me' at those around him. I was repelled and yet annoyingly curious. He threatened the natural order of our class and our carefully won reputation. We disliked him on sight. He was not one of us.

In the art lesson he dashed off bright dramatic pictures that made my work look over-worked and fussy. His careless ease with his talent offended my diligence and I could not help being jealous of his confidence and indifference to criticism. We could all 'take it or leave it' as far as he was concerned.

On the yard he soon became involved in a fight and had to be dragged away, his knuckles cut and reddened by the affray. One Monday morning he turned up with a still livid red cut over one eyebrow that had caught together with stitches. He glowered at us almost challenging someone to ask what had happened. No one did.

The days wore on and an uneasy truce was established. The younger girls in the year below us threw admiring glances at him and tittered at his approach. He knew that he was turning their heads; revelling in their adoration. During our lessons he attempted to mock those around him who asked for clarification or an explanation, undermining the philosophy of open discussion and working through problems together which our teachers had always encouraged. I had encountered huge problems trying to understand the principle of negative numbers. Mr Lloyd, our respected Maths teacher would patiently find another way to explain the concept again, drawing examples on the blackboard until a glimmer of understanding began to settle in my brain.

I could hear his muffled sounds of contempt behind me, and was furious to know that it had had an effect on me. 'Why let him get under your skin? Just ignore him!' But it was easier said than done. His influence was powerful; he found weaknesses and manipulated them.

I found myself flattered to be fancied by a boy in the year above us. Ian shyly asked me out for a date and I was excited by his earnest request. He introduced me to music that I had never listened to before. I went to meet his family and we sat on the floor in his lounge listening to the protest songs of Bob Dylan, 'We shall not be Moved' and 'The Times they are a changing'. I felt completely out of my depth having not a clue what the song meant. I dare not admit that I didn't understand the lyrics nor like Dylan's raspy, raw voice with his breathless wheezing of the harmonica accompanying each song. Somehow to have criticised the artist would have included Ian in the criticism for his choice in music and also exposed my ignorance. I kept shtoom and nodded thoughtfully throughout his droning, performance. Happily he also liked Joan Baez. Her clear, pure voice held me in awe. Although I didn't fully understand the references of civil protest or know all the details about the tragedy of 'Birmingham Sunday' I loved her voice and thought her exotic and beautiful as I read the blurb on the LP cover and murmured my accompaniment, 'and the choirs kept singing of freedom'.

141

As my relationship with Ian grew so I began to dimly understand that many American veterans were protesting against the Vietnam War and that a Civil Rights Act of 1964 had been signed by the new President Lyndon Johnson who I hadn't really thought about. He wasn't film star quality, like Kennedy had been, so I hadn't paid much attention.

But Ian discussed predetermination and Christianity, God and the Universe. I began to grow restless, worried about how serious the relationship was getting. I didn't want to be so closed in. I was just fifteen. I wasn't sure how much I actually fancied him. We held hands, and kissed chastely but anything more physical embarrassed me. I liked the idea of having a boyfriend and being adored, but commitment was not something that I could envisage. Suddenly I realised that there was no easy way to break it off and I didn't have the courage or skills to do it properly. I could be noble in discussions but in reality I was a coward.

Meanwhile school was keeping me busy. My fourth form report had been generous with praise which had delighted me. I was committed to the school hockey team and we had enjoyed inter-school match success. My list of clubs, societies and teams section included: 'Chess Club, House Choral Speaking, Duke of Edinburgh award scheme, House Netball team, House Hockey XI, and School Hockey XI. The teachers had awarded me A's for attainment and effort and my form master, John Elliott,,had said that the report was 'exemplary'. No wonder I had been on such a high.

Senacre had been quite progressive for its day by providing its fifth and sixth formers a Common Room in which to socialise and study in the wing away from the main school building. They had set up a pool table, comfortable easy chairs and low coffee tables. It made us feel very special and so grown up. I became House Captain, and the Room 1 committee member for the common room. By now we had lost a large proportion of our fellow class mates as they had left school for work in the last term of our fourth year. I now shared my interests in studies and the games field with Linda. After school we would often go back to her place to carry on studying as she lived just

142

across the road from school. We both enjoyed Human Biology and were team players in the school team but competitors in the inter-house matches. Linda and I became firm friends. We walked her dog, poured over fashion catalogues, went swimming together, and just spent time enjoying each other's company.

In the spring of that year the school had a special play written for it by our Head of English John Hipkin. He had devised a 'theatre in the round' production, with the subject being the 'Massacre of Peterloo'. We had only understood the concept of drama and plays being set on a stage. The school productions in the past had been nothing like the epic drama that he created for us. But first he ensured that we understood the historical background about the Lancashire workers and their families who gathered in Manchester to listen to their leader Henry Hunt. That they were there to demand the right of representation in Parliament but then, without warning, they were attacked by the Manchester yeomanry resulting in mayhem and death for hundreds of men, women and children. It made a huge impression on us all. We felt so special to have been involved in an original piece. We had also recreated a piece of history.

But now in the Autumn term of 1965 Miss Jean Oldershaw was our form mistress. She took me to one side in the common room.

"Your report this term has been excellent. We have been looking at the possibility of you transferring to the Grammar School in order that you can take an 'A' Level course. How do you feel about that?"

The truth was that the whole idea frightened me. I had gloried in being successful at Senacre. I was a big fish in a little pond. The transfer would see me being a little fish in a very big pond. How would I cope? I didn't want to leave!

"Yes. I would love that." I smiled back at her.

"Well then, I will write to your parents and contact the Grammar School."

I nodded back enthusiastically; my heart thumped tightly. What could I say? She was so sure that it was the right thing to do. I hoped that the Grammar School would say no, but my pride wanted it to say yes.

Once again I was being pulled in two directions just as I had been when I took the 13 plus exam. I would have to leave my special friends, Linda, Grahame and John. We were like the three Musketeers, only four; always together, sharing things.

The spring term of 1966 came and went. We took the mock exams and I panicked once again. My report reflected my lack of confidence under pressure.

Jean Oldershaw discussed things with me.

"The Grammar school will look again at the transfer. If you do pass these exams they will probably want to take you. We'll just see how things go for now."

I mutely agreed. I had let people down. Not only had I hurt Ian, not able to tell him face to face that I didn't want to carry on, letting him find out that I wasn't interested and had someone else in mind. And now here I was making a mess of the mocks.

At home things were rumbling along. Heather had gained her Diploma of Art from the college and had first worked in Ashford with an advertising agency. She was now living in a small bedsit in West Norwood working for the Decca Record Company. She was successful and living, what I perceived to be, a Bohemian lifestyle. When I had gone up to visit her, she showed me around her little room with its small kitchenette behind a curtain, a small wardrobe, a settee that could be turned into a bed, a table with her record player, books on a shelf. And then she cooked tea for us which included savoury rice. It was so exotic. A 'Room at the Top' with style. I had never eaten rice like that before. We just had sweet rice puddings at home. Dad always insisted in running his knife around the edge of the dish to scrape off browned crust.

"That the best bit!" He'd gleefully say.

But rice with a salad, and a salad that had green peppers in it! I'd never heard of them. She showed me some record sleeves that she had designed and I was in awe. Seriously impressed. She now lived an independent life and even had black friends at work. It was quite surreal. Quite light years away from Maidstone and home. Mrs Fine, her landlady looked strangely normal and homely. It was quite odd.

Heather also had tickets for us to see Joan Baez in concert at the Royal Albert Hall. I was so looking forward to it.

Although Heather had moved away, I didn't for some reason get upgraded to have her bedroom. Perhaps Mum and Dad thought that her move was just temporary. I have never really considered why I stayed in my little room. Ian had made me a bookcase in his wood-work class so I was now able to put my books on shelves instead of being piled up in the three quarter wardrobe that was foreshortened due to its position over the stairs. Now that I was in the fifth form we could have some variation from the set uniform. I made myself a summer dress from some striped navy and white cotton material. I used the dining room table to pin out the pattern. Mum and Dad now had a new second hand square table. I don't know where it came from. Perhaps it was Gran's or Aunty Betty's. It was an improvement on the last one as we were able to extend it by drawing out two leaves either side to elongate it into a rectangle. They also had a new sideboard with drawers for the cutlery, tablecloths and other family paraphernalia. Dad commandeered the left-hand side cupboard for his 'bits and pieces', which included his technical drawing pens, oil and water colour paints, mixing palette and fine squirrel-hair brushes.

Life was a little calmer with just the three of us at home but my staying over at Linda's after school, and then neglecting to let Mum know, led to some serious rows. Mum was working more hours as a domestic to earn some extra money. Things were getting more expensive each year and although there was one less mouth to feed somehow the money still did not stretch far enough. Dad's Bond had long since died and gone to the motor home in the sky, so he purchased a second hand, two-seater, powder-blue Austin Healey in its place and he had purchased a small transistor Bush radio with its large dial, to find the stations, complete with a carrying handle.

There had been strong words and recriminations about the choice of vehicle and the cost. Our Queen Ann style cooker had been replaced with a Belling cooker with four rings and we had a small 'fridge at long last, but otherwise the house still stayed in its 1940-50 guise. Around us our neighbours were acquiring cars, the road outside our house became a race track. On a Friday and Saturday night the drunken revellers continued to weave an uncertain path back to their homes. It became noisier during the day and the night with a mixture of cars, motor bikes, barking dogs and the shouts and arguments of 'The Century' pub clientele. I hated coming home from school to find an empty house waiting for me. By then some of the neighbours who had been on the estate from the beginning had moved on. Our immediate neighbours left and were replaced by a friendly couple with two little girls.

It was around that time that I found out about an old school friend who had fallen pregnant during a one-night stand. She had been thrown out of her family home by her furious father and had to spend her confinement in a hostel for unmarried mothers. Whispered rumour had it that the baby was going to be black. I was horrified by the catastrophe and what the future would hold for her. For a while all my cares seemed quite insignificant. A glimpse into the real world was frightening.

At home Dad was still endeavouring to acquire bits of copper and brass to finish his engine. I would be required to pump a little lever to raise the water pressure in the boiler to see if it was leak proof so that he could then fire up the boiler and test for steam pressure. Each Sunday he would don his MR hat, which I called his Mister Hat, but actually stood for the Model Railway, and put on his short engineers jacket for his day over the other side of the park to run the model steam trains for the public. The circular track had been extended to a figure eight and the little brick bridge had been ceremoniously opened. Vandalism had damaged the track sometimes by nature and other times by man. Once a gale had upended a large tree which had smashed across the track and at other times the model engineers had arrived to find the lengths of the track had been stolen; it had been torn up and sold for scrap.

Weekends were sometimes spent meeting up with Linda or Grahame, or Mum and I would go along to Gran's to do some jobs for her. Other times I would dig the garden, do some weeding or try to tidy up the house. Mum had always been haphazard in her approach to housework but it started to worry me. I was conscious of how our home would look in someone else's eyes.

"If they are real friends they would want to see you, not how the house looks." Mum rebuked me, but as soon as she was out of the house I would make a start on the kitchen, wiping down the cupboards and then tidying up around Dad's latest project. Sometimes I would use a small paint brush in an attempt to dust his model of the Golden Hind, which he had made from slivers of wood, string for the rigging, tiny pieces of metal and lacquered paper for the sails.

I knew that Mum was right but then I also knew that I made judgements when I visited my friend's houses. With Grahame we used to roar with laugher about his Mum who worked at the fish shop in Earl Street. She always seemed to have some fish steaming on her cooker.

"Excuse the pong, its fish again." he would say as we creased up, giggling uncontrollably. His Dad always seemed to have some new project on the go and had just installed a huge mast in the garden to satisfy his ham-radio hobby.

In those days we didn't use our bedrooms as retreats; we spent our time sprawled out on the lounge floor, listening to records, drinking coffee and talking about the latest film or record, what was happening at school, exchanging gossip, and what we wanted to do with our lives or promising to do some revision which always gave way to more important to discuss. We would arrive with books and texts and leave again with the books still unopened.

Then to my dismay I found that I had more than an odd sprinkling of spots and blackheads. Each month, as soon as one throbbing lump had subsided and the area finally calm down; another would suddenly appear and start the process off all over again. I started to apply more matt stick foundation cream to cover them. We mostly copied the Mary Quant look, attempting a pout with pale lipstick and lashings of black eye liner and mascara, but I had decided to grow my mousey brown hair longer like Jean Shrimpton, waiting impatiently to see how it looked at shoulder length.

Finally we took our exams and waited for the results to be declared that summer. We knew that we could stay on for another year to take further 'O' levels but I did not know whether I would be going to the Grammar or not. I didn't even discuss it with Linda or Grahame. When the results came through I found that I had passed all the 'O' levels and most of the 'easier' CSE at grade 1, with the strange exception of cookery which I passed at 'O' level yet was only awarded low grade 4 in the CSE which rather confounded the idea of parallel marking. We found to our sorrow that John had been accepted for a place at the Boys Grammar to begin an 'A' Level course and so the four became just three.

Linda, Grahame and I went into the sixth form together as prefects. Jean Oldershaw drew me to one side and carefully explained to me that the Grammar School had decided to wait to see if I had been successful in the exams, and although I had passed them all they had informed her that they had decided that it was now too late to transfer. I didn't quite know how to receive the news. What was the appropriate response? On one hand I was furious that they had gone back on their word and yet was so relieved that I didn't have to go. Probably I wasn't able to disguise my happiness at being able to stay with my friends and the teachers whom I trusted. Anyway to soften the 'blow' she said that the school had full confidence in me and had decided to make me Head Girl.

We settled back into the easy routine. I was to take a further five 'O' levels, English Literature, Religious Knowledge, History, Human Biology and Art. Now we were also invited to John Elliot's little town house in College Road in Maidstone to meet as a 'select' discussion group. We talked about religion, politics, discrimination, our hopes and fears for the future, reviewed books that we had just read and believed ourselves to be incredibly grownup. After all we were sixteen going on seventeen, and hadn't we been told how 'mature' we were? John Hipkin, his friend, said that we were now able to appreciate works of literature such as of DH Lawrence's Lady Chatterley's Lover. We read the 1st World War poetry of Wilfred Owen, discussed the British Imperialism, communism, argued about racism, discrimination against travelling people, the Holocaust, World famine, unions and the rights of the working man and woman. Were we being indoctrinated? No, I don't think so. They were providing the opportunity to vocalise and order our thoughts; to listen to counter arguments and think things through. It was a time of 'Cathy Come Home' and the angry young man. We were safely sheltered from the effects of such fractured violent lives and so our understanding of the lives of others came from the newspapers that our parents brought into our homes and our opinions reflected their opinions. We had heard that some Rock and Roll stars smoked 'pot', and that there was some gang crime in the big cities and the notorious Kray twins were trouble in London, but for us, apart from Grahame's Dad smoking cigarettes and my Dad enjoying his pipe we had no contact with drugs or criminality.

Our morals were set by a fear of condemnation and a need for respectability. Those who 'two timed' were not to be trusted, you shouldn't go 'all the way' until you were married or at least engaged to be married, and white lies were only permissible if they protected someone's feelings. We were so quaint, untested and untried, thinking we had all the answers. Everything was so clear then; there was no room for compromise.

We were intrigued about the Royal family, respected our politicians, except of course people like Profumo, thought that the police did a very good job, that there was no need to swear, we had the best national football team and some poor 'countries' like Africa needed our aid. Oh goodness, we didn't even know the difference between a country and a continent, let alone where half these places were in Africa and the rest of the world. We viewed communism as a benign Christian life style, sharing and caring for all. We were oblivious to the violent Cultural Revolution in China, as we sat there smugly drinking our coffee in what we considered to be avant-garde fashion; these things were way beyond our periscope on life.

Free love, sex, rock and roll, drugs not on our Shepway estate! I had never eaten a pizza or tasted Dandelion and Burdock. Our innocence was quite intact.

Most of our points of reference still came from the old set of 1950's encyclopaedias sitting on the shelf in the front room. I still had my 'Gollywog' Robertson's marmalade badges at home, and my cigarette cards and prized stamp collection; in fact I was still avidly collecting stamps. In my mind's eye I thought that most Africans lived in mud huts, pounding maize in large wooden bowls with a heavy pole; that the wide-hatted Chinese worked as coolies in the rice paddies, that most Americans lived on ranches wearing their Stetsons as they rounded up the cattle, that somehow there still were Indians out on the plains making rounded tepees from the skins of the buffalo, that the Australians were all descended from convicts and were cared for by the Flying Doctor who came when called on an old wind-up wireless system; the native Aboriginals still went on walkabouts, and that we English were more advanced and civilised than most other countries although I acknowledged that the Romans had built straight roads and knew a thing or two about baths, natural springs and hot spa water.

We had no idea of the term 'offensive language' except about swearing in public and had tittered when Audrey Hepburn as Eliza Doolittle said 'not bloody likely' in the My Fair Lady film. We benignly called people who had any disability 'spastic', as we routinely collected money for the Spastic Society, and those with mental health problems we called 'loony' or 'barmy'. Linda's Mum worked night shifts at the local Kent County Council Lunatic Asylum at Oakwood Hospital, which was up the Tonbridge Road although she never said anything about her work on waking from her afternoon nap in the arm chair when we got back from school.

Hardly anyone I knew had been abroad, except my Aunty Joan who went to Madeira, and Heather, who eventually managed to get out to Greece and spent two weeks in Athens. Dad's memories of foreign parts were confined to the unsavoury naval ports, docklands, and his war time spent in Egypt. He had a very low opinion of the Arabs saying that they were not to be trusted, were sly and treated woman badly, and so our prejudices and ignorance was shared by all those around us. Dad used to joke about the Sunny Smiles charity booklets

150

that routinely came round each Christmas. You were supposed to tear out a picture of a smiling black child and give some money in return.

"I'm sure that's the same face that I saw ten years ago!" he would say, "should have thought that she would have grown up by now." He winked at me, making me laugh.

And yet I have no recollection of the North South divide and any antagonism against those who lived in Scotland, Wales or the north of the country despite our southern accents being criticised by Father Payne when Dad's father came to visit us from Nottingham. I knew we were poor so I couldn't understand it when he talked about us 'soft Southerners living off milk and honey', but I saw Mum's face and knew that she was not happy.

That autumn Dad and I went along on our usual Saturday afternoon to Grans' house to watch Doctor Who, when we saw the news about the previous day's nightmare disaster of a landslide at Aberfan in Wales. We watched as the reporter spoke of the coal slag heap slipping and sliding down to cover a little school and a couple of nearby houses killing over one hundred children. People were wading through the sludge of liquid coal. They had tried to dig out the children. I was horrified as it brought back memories of our neighbours who had been buried under the hot tar some years earlier. Years before the quick sand episode in the film 'Ice Cold in Alex' had caused me sleepless nights, and now a real disaster was being played out on the news; I shuddered at the thought of such an agonising, suffocating, death.

At the end of the Autumn term my school report continued to make me swell with pride, Norman Evans had written as usual in red pen, in his almost illegible style, opposite the page containing the teachers 'A' grades and comments, 'Exemplary. She does herself, and us as a school, the greatest credit.'

I was still passionate about my prowess on the hockey field. Linda and I spent more and more time perfecting our skills on the pitch, so much so that Jean Oldershaw invited us both to play for the Maidstone town team. We became members of the successful Maidstone Ladies Hockey team. Our pitch was over at South Park and we used the pavilion for our changing room, enjoying the

151

camaraderie of the other players, and were regularly picked to play for the team each Saturday.

And by the following spring my heroine, Elizabeth Thatcher our form teacher, had generously written,

'an outstanding record of quietly consistent determination and achievement. Perhaps the happiest point is that Julia has been so successful and yet still remains one of the pleasantest pupils I have ever met.'

To which Norman Evans added, 'The consistency of these reports is almost unparalleled in my experience'.

To say I was pleased would be an understatement; they made my heart soar.

Linda and I continued to study together, testing our understanding and knowledge in Human Biology; drawing diagrams of the digestive system, naming the bones of the body, remembering the mnemonic for the sensory nerves, 'On old Olympic Towering tops a Finn and German viewed some hops'.

We had also had to think of what we were going to do after leaving Senacre.

Linda had decided that she was going to do an 'A' level correspondence course at home whilst Grahame and I toyed with the idea of doing a couple of 'A' levels at the local Medway College of Further Education over in Chatham as we had both decided to go in for teaching. I wanted to take two subjects, Art and English. We applied for a place at the college. The answer came back that they did not regard taking just two subjects in the one year as a full-time course and that we would have to study for at least three subjects. As for my choice of Art and English, this would not be available. I could take English but had to choose another two others from a selection of History, Geography, or Economics. I was mortified. Those pupils in the Grammar school had been able to take two years studying at 'A' Level taking two or three subjects of their choice but I would have to take an additional two subjects that I had little interest or ability in. I discussed my concerns with Elizabeth Thatcher. She was as disappointed as I was.

"It almost appears as if they are trying to put you off going." She murmured. "Don't let them do that."

But I was worried. Did I really want to go? Should I think of something else? How could I take those subjects when I had no talent for them? And what would happen if I failed? I was scared.

During the art lessons Brian Cannell introduced quick line drawings encouraging me to capture a figure using just a few defining lines. He wrote:

GCE   Preparations

Figure drawings

'As much practice as possible in quick 10 minute sketches. The main aim is to show you understand the tensions in the figure involved in the action, and of course good proportioning in your drawing.

Watch the angles created by:-the shoulders, arms, slope of head, legs, level of hips etc.....

Try to get "vitality" into the line, exaggerate actions to produce this "Dynamic effect...'

He continued to outline the importance of perspective and to detail pointers for the longer drawing task which would take one and half hours to compete. This support was invaluable. I was to draw anyone as quickly as I could and not go back to re-work the piece. Linda, Grahame and Mum and even the cat at home became my impromptu models, "just for a couple of minutes no more" I would plead. The first sketches were very poor but gradually I began to improve, almost capturing a pose as I attempted to make myself work faster.

By now I had embarked upon a disastrous relationship with the unstable David. Drawn towards him, against my better judgement, not even able to explain to myself why I had allowed it to start. In my sketch book I still have a one of him lounging outstretched, staring disdainfully back at me; his pointed winkle-picker shoes resting on a desk. His dark moody manner repelled me, his swaggering posturing found him no friends in the sixth form and yet we carried on. I knew that Mum disapproved. He was trouble with a big 'T', as she said.

Somehow I think that she knew his mother and there were concerns about his violent behaviour at home, his aggressive attitude to his family, and that it he was mixing with a bad crowd.

"I shouldn't wonder if the police don't get involved one day," Mum sniffed.

It wasn't as if we had a good time together; most of the time we hardly spoke. Finally it was all over. I'm not sure if he got tired of, trying to make me go 'further', and ostracizing me from my friends, but it was quite a relief not trying to be someone that I wasn't. Perhaps he decided that the challenge wasn't worth it. Whatever it was my life then resumed the normality that I had missed. I once more enjoyed the comfort of friends around me. Why is it that at times we venture too close to the candle flame? Looking back I was lucky to have escaped without any damage, just a dented ego and some serious doubts about my flawed judgements.

In the RE lessons John Elliott continued to challenge us to commit the Gospel according to St Matthew to memory. Whole chunks of chapter and verse were required by the GCE examiners to show that we had indeed studied the New Testament and understood that which we had read. He teased us when we expressed doubts about our ability to pass.

"Well if you pass it because I am such a wonderful teacher and if you fail, then it shows that you were just poor students!"

"That's not fair!"

"Of course it's not," he refused to be serious, his throaty laughter and long nicotine fingers betraying his addiction to cigarettes.

During the previous year Mr Lloyd, our Maths teacher had realised that it was not my strongest subject and whenever I had voiced my qualms about passing he had always calmed me by saying.

"You can always take it again next year."

I don't know who was more surprised when I passed first time, him or me. I remember him saying with his quiet humour, "perhaps they (the examiners) were having a good day when they marked yours."

And so the exams drew near and then the time to leave school arrived.

There was a brief period between the exams and the end of term that were filled with odd 'time-filling' moments. Linda and I decided to paint Jean Oldershaw's little changing room next to the girl's shower room a brilliant 'Day-Glo' orange. The colour on the outside of the tin hadn't appeared to be as bright as it was when we finally applied it. To her credit she accepted the change with good humour, and didn't even raise an eyebrow when we also decided to paint little black dancing figures, as a kind of frieze, around the walls at waist height.

We learnt a few ballroom steps during a lunchtime period having only ever learnt to dance Scottish reels in the designated PE sessions. To this day I can only lead and do that very badly. Norman Evans also decided to take us for a few sessions to prepare us for a world away from school. The sessions didn't make much sense to me. Perhaps the topics that he chose were off my radar. They didn't include the scandal of the Rolling Stones being raided for drugs or the affair between Mick Jagger and Marion Faithful that had involved a Mars Bar. The sexual references had baffled me, but I pretended to be suitably shocked at the disclosure, whilst all the time wondering what an earth they had done.

I still avidly watched 'Top of the Pops' when along at Gran's house, studiously ignoring her when she said that she couldn't understand any of the words,

"And just look at their long hair! They need some scissors taken to them!"

Thankfully she didn't know about Jimmy Hendrix and his escapade with his guitar. She would have been suitably scandalised at such behaviour. I was shocked about the fire on stage, about the damage to a piece of equipment. I wasn't my father's daughter for nothing. Tools of the trade were to be treated reverently at all times. So I certainly didn't want to have to justify something that I couldn't understand, which might have also called into question my defence of the groups whom I followed. The Beatles new album Sgt. Pepper's Lonely Hearts Club Band had already confused me, with any references to hallucinogenic drugs having passed me by. Then the announced death of Brian Epstein had the newspapers hinting that there was more scandal to unfold.

As June arrived we watched Billy Jean King hold centre court at Wimbledon, finally demonstrating that women's tennis was exciting and just as entertaining as the men's game.

 And so July heralded the end of an era. We enjoyed a 'Barn Dance' which I was relieved to find didn't involve dressing up, but the reverse, dressing down. At home I had started to wear stretch slacks, the bottoms of the trouser had a strap under the foot to keep the trouser pulled straight. We didn't quite go barefoot as Sandie Shaw did during her performance of 'Puppet on a string' during the Eurovision contest but things were definitely beginning to relax. It was still taboo to eat anything in the street except fish and chips from newspaper late at night, which I was allowed to do with Dad after going to the pictures.

Dad and I were going to the Granada one evening to see 'the latest James Bond film 'You Only Live Twice'. I was self consciously wearing for the first time my 'love at first sight', very first pair of kitten-heeled black patent shoes purchased from the Golden Boot in Gabriel's Hill earlier that afternoon. I was still a little unsure about walking in them but as I was linking arms with Dad I seemed to be managing without drawing attention to myself. The queue moved forward and stopped, surged forward and stopped as the uniformed doorman allowed so many people through at a time to purchase their tickets. Finally we were waved on and I waited as Dad got our tickets. As I went to follow him across the foyer I realised with horror that I couldn't move. My heel had got stuck in the rubber matting at the entrance. Dad looked back to see why I wasn't with him and then turned to help me out of my shoe as the doorman attempted to pull my shoe from the matting, but it was stuck fast. I had visions of the ignominy of having to go in just wearing one shoe. Finally he managed to prise it free and handed it back to me with a flourish. I could hardly manage to thank him as by this time my cheeks were blazing in acute mortification.

At home I now tuned in to new pop music station Radio One and sang along with the Beatles latest hit 'All you need is Love'. Mum was still working as a domestic help and I had been accepted at Medway College to do the one year's course studying three 'A' levels; English, History and Economics. Mum and I sent away for Teacher's Training College prospectuses to see which subject qualifications they required.

The last day at school arrived and we took in our Autograph albums to be signed by members of the staff and of course our friends

John Hipkin, who always commented on my serious demeanour wrote, 'Best Wishes, Julia, for your future happiness. Keep smiling!' He just couldn't help himself. As for John Elliott he decided to write, 'A Reference - This young lady looks, but is no lady. She is rude and always on the attack- a masochists delight. Since I am a masochist I thoroughly recommend her.' My fellow pupils managed to scribble various smutty poems full of innuendo, demonstrating typical silly school -boy humour, and then the day drew to a close.

We walked out of the school and I never went back.

From the top: Playing chess at Senacre School, in the garden with Niggy and on holiday in Wales with Mum, Dad and Aunt Sally in 1964

Back row: Me with my boyfriend Ian, Uncle Alan and his parents. *Front row*: Aunty Betty and Gran

Me at the seaside with Mum, then me (far right) with the Guides at summer camp still wearing the awful 'dyed' shorts

Maths class at Senacre School
From left back row: Grahame, John S and John M
Next row: Barbara, Pat and me
By the window: Stephen and Mr Lloyd

Me revising in the garden

Top: Senacre School Common Room

Above: Line drawing of David

Left: Line drawing of Grahame

161

Chapter 4   1967 – 1968 Leaving home

The summer of 1967 slowly passed by. If it was a 'Summer of Love' then it by passed everyone whom I knew. The legacy of the 1950's limited my experiences; we were still bound by the traditions of our family, a culture of class, and the limitations of money. The hippy culture was a term that we vaguely associated with a new American fashion trend. Long hair for both girls and boys, perhaps wearing a bandanna, flared trousers with a slit at the sides with a piece of material inserted in the side seam and for the men, having long sideburns and a big Che Guevara moustache although I hadn't the slightest idea who Che Guevara was, having only seen the art posters in the shops and not thought anymore about him. I knew that there was talk in the newspapers and on the television about LSD and cannabis and it was said the pop stars had been in smoking 'pot or weed' but a hippy lifestyle was something that I still considered to be a strange foreign phenomena. I hadn't even attended a disco. Had the Glastonbury Festival was started by then? I can't remember but it wasn't until 1968 that I went to see the musical Hair, and, due to my incomprehension of the lyrics, and the flash of dazzling stage lighting at an opportune moment, I left as uncorrupted as when I arrived.

Linda and I went picking raspberries on a farm near Langley to get some extra cash. It was a frustrating job that required a good technique, not to squash the fruit, and also to avoid the stinging nettles and brambles that seemed to have planted themselves willy-nilly between each raspberry cane. Having stupidly worn a light summer skirt and not a pair of slacks I came home with my arms and legs covered in raised itchy lumps and unsightly scratches and little monetary reward. I didn't go there again.

We also embarked on a Friday night forty-four mile walk for the Cheshire Homes Charity in Mote Park. Again I think that it was Linda who suggested it. We set off at dusk with a large assortment of people, young and old. Some experienced walkers were competing against the clock and then there were those, like us, who just wanted to raise money for the charity. We were to walk throughout the night. After twenty odd miles in the darkness I was ready to call it a day, but Linda was made of sterner stuff and cajoled me to keep going. Our arrival back in Maidstone early the following morning was met by the official photographer from The Kent Messenger. Linda and I were, amazingly, the first girls back. Our photo was posted in the paper. Amongst all my childhood bits and pieces I still have a tatty copy, celebrating the achievement. By the time I reached home my feet were painfully cramped. But to my amazement, Dad carefully massaged them so thoroughly, that, by his expert rubbing and squeezing, my toes began to gradually unlock. Later that day I was able to walk along with him to Gran's to watch the latest episode of 'Dixon of Dock Green' without the slightest discomfort.

If I wasn't hanging out with Linda then I would meet up with Grahame. One day we went up to London. His brother worked as a technician with the BBC so he invited us up to visit him there at the Art Deco style round glass-fronted Television Centre in Wood Lane. The BBC had been working on broadcasting the programmes in colour. It was the first time that I had seen a television programme in colour and I remember being very impressed. Somehow it was so different to the films shown in glorious 'Technicolor' at the cinema. There was something quite intimate and very special about it.

My routine at home was unchanged as I waited for the Medway College course to begin. I was in a kind of limbo. I had already lost touch with most of the people at Senacre. We had been such a small intimate 6th form group. John, having still a year to go at the Boys Grammar, I saw occasionally, but apart from Linda and Grahame my social world had shrunk. If I went down to the town with Mum and saw any of my contemporaries who had left in the 4th year it was as if they inhabited another world. They were now working, 'going steady', had their sights set on marriage and a house, a car and a family. They had an air of maturity that a wage packet at the end of each week afforded them. Did I imagine it or did they regard me with some amusement. An ill-dressed oddity. Had aspirations quite above herself. Stuck up. Always was too serious. I felt quite uncomfortable, barely able to exchange pleasantries; to engage in small talk. The awkwardness was painfully obvious. The conversation was stilted, meaningless unconnected words. Questions asked to fill the void.

"Oh hello".

"How are ya?"

"Long time, no see!"

"Going steady now.

"Do you remember him? No?"

"And you?"

"Really, college?"

"What will you do then?"

They drifted off, their laughter hung in the air as a kind of rebuke.

I continued to window shop, gazing at things that I still could not afford to buy and wondered all over again whether I was doing the right thing. I envied those who seemed so self-assured, dressed in the latest style. They seemed to be living their lives, whilst I still was waiting for mine to begin. And yet I didn't want marriage and a family. I watched those harassed girls, pushing a pram, with a toddler struggling to keep up, lagging behind and whining. No. I didn't want that. But to go away on a foreign holiday, buy a new dress for the Saturday night disco, breeze up to London and visit Carnaby Street.

Secret images crept into my mind, day-dreaming images that I would have denied if challenged. I almost managed to convince myself that I had not dreamt those shallow and materialistic thoughts, and yet, and yet, I was just seventeen, yearning to flaunt my youth.

My pride of what I could be, of what I could achieve, quelled my rebellious cravings.

165

During any sunny period I snatched moments in the garden to sunbath endeavouring to acquire a 'sun kissed' appearance but as the sunny periods were so infrequent I would lie out far too long whilst the sun was shining and then turn lobster pink before peeling. I still did most of the gardening, planting out runner beans and developing a healthy strawberry patch and further up the garden towards the rhubarb I had some raspberry canes. The bindweed became my chief enemy as it wound and tangled its way up and through other plants. And to attempt to tear it away usually resulted in it snapping the very plant that I was struggling to free from its tight embrace. Whilst the large white open bell 'Grandmother, grandmother pop out of bed' flowers looked so delightful if I left one tiny piece of white root in the soil it would manage to grow a complete Triffid and come back stronger than ever. It covertly crept under the garden path, hiding until it had gained strength, so that I could never completely eradicate it. On days when the garden hedge needed to be cut and trimmed with ineffective shears I would light a bonfire and feed the flames until most of the debris had been consumed, and then I would go inside taking the bonfire smell with me.

Sometimes Linda would come down with her friendly old scruffy dog Sally and we would go for a walk in Mote Park or we would meet up with Grahame and go to his house in Northumberland Avenue. We discussed how to earn some money to help us pay for the bus fare to Medway College as we could not get a grant for travelling expenses. Linda had already found a waitressing job over at the Great Danes Hotel on the Ashford Road near Leeds Castle and asked if I wanted her to find out if they had any other vacancies. I needed to get a weekend job as I would be at college during the week. She found that they wanted someone on Sundays from 7 o'clock in the morning until 7 o'clock in the evening and they would pay 2/6 an hour. I immediately applied for the job, not wanting to miss any opportunity. It was arranged that a mini bus from The Great Danes would pick me up at the end of School Lane at Willington Street at quarter to seven along with other fellow workers and I would then catch the same mini bus back home. A uniform would also be provided.

Finally the Autumn term arrived. Grahame and I caught the first bus into town and then another one out to the college. It crawled slowly up the Bluebell Hill past the outcrops of stark white chalk leaving the town and the surrounding Weald of Kent far below us.

I don't know what we expected to find. Perhaps we thought that we would be treated in a similar fashion to the one that we had experienced at Senacre. That was our first mistake. The lecturers were not impressed with us and happy to make that quite obvious to us. First we came from a Secondary Modern school and then to compound our dubious pedigree, we also lived on a council estate. The first English lecture began with a distribution of papers including a reading list and a synopsis of the one year 'A' Level syllabus that we were to study. We would be looking at Chaucer's Canterbury Tales, with special reference to The Prologue and The Clerk's Tale. We would study two Shakespeare plays; The Tempest and Othello. We would be reading the novel A Portrait of an Artist as a Young Man and examining the poetry of Milton and Tennyson.

It didn't get us off to a good start when one of the lecturers returned Grahame's information sheet back to him with corrections and a red line through the 'e' in his name as if Grahame didn't know how to spell his own name. It was humiliating. Our fellow students included a couple of mature students and there were others who had previously taken the 'A' level exam and failed so they were a year older than Grahame and I. One of the older students, who lived in one of the large private houses in Willington Street, was the son of someone Mum knew from the Mother's Union. His crisp, clipped vowels and confident air spoke of money and privilege which made me feel shy and ignorant in his company.

We were also given the books and paper work for the 'A' level History and Economics course, which filled me with a potent mixture of dread and apprehension. All that work in one year and with lecturers who looked as if they would have been happier if we had not been there.

I think our fits of giggles and laughter on the way home on the top deck of the bus had more to do with relieving the tensions of the day rather than finding anything humorous.

I had also acquired another boyfriend, Chris. We didn't have that much in common but he was different to friends that I had mixed with at school. First he was working at as an apprentice and secondly he owned a car, which put him into a different league. Whilst Linda and I were still playing hockey with the Maidstone Ladies on a Saturday, he played rugby during the afternoon. My Sunday was taken up with the job at The Great Danes so my time to spend with Chris was rather limited.

I found it hard to study on my own without the structure of school around me. I had always been a 'last minute merchant' needing to have a deadline before I could galvanise myself into action. But the demands of the three 'A' levels became too much. I felt at sea with the syllabus in both History and Economics and didn't know what to do.

Each Sunday morning it would be still dark as I went to get ready for work. Pulling on the ill fitting, short-skirted shiny cheap uniform and then a thick duffle coat to keep out the chill wind I trudged off down the road to wait for the mini bus to appear. My first shift at seven began with breakfast room service. A large silver tray had to be carried up the wide carpeted stairs to the bedrooms. The tray was piled high with a silver teapot, milk jug, sugar bowl with tongs, cereal bowl, heavy duty silver cutlery, toast rack, a selection of individual marmalades, boiled eggs or a plated breakfast covered with a silver dome, and a cup and saucer. How it all managed to fit on the tray was a feat in itself but so was carrying the tray up the stairs without a mishap. By the second stair level I could feel my arms giving way as the weight began to make my muscles shake. It was a much as I could do to manage to knock at the door, shifting the weight to just one arm underneath the tray and call "Room service!"

The rule was never to enter the room in case the male guest 'took advantage' so I had to wait until the occupant was sufficiently roused from his slumber to open the door and then to hand the tray over.

After room service had been completed I then started on breakfast service in the main dining room. The chefs were querulous and impatient. I think that one of the qualifications to becoming a chef had to be having a short fuse and a nasty, fiery temper. I would swing the door open and enter the kitchen to pick up the next order, but the waitress was supposed to know instinctively which plate was destined for what table.

"This one!

There!

Hurry up!

Table four!

Here!

For fuck's sake.

Two full English!

Go now!"

The staccato orders were barked out. As the older waitresses were used to the shouts and swearing they took it all in their stride. But on that first day I nearly jumped out of my skin at the anger and aggression. It took some weeks, but after a while I too became immune to the squabbles, suggestive remarks and lewd posturing of the chefs, pretending not to hear or see them.

After the stint in the dining room I would make a start on serving mid-morning refreshments at ten-thirty at the poolside lounge. This time coffee, tea, cold drinks, cakes, biscuits and pastries were on offer.

As that service grew to an end we would start to napkin fold and set out the glasses and cutlery for lunch in the leisure area restaurant. I had still not had a break and would not be able to sit down until lunch was over at two o'clock, when I would be able to have a half hour break to have my own lunch, a luke-warm roast dinner, which was provided by the hotel.

Then it would be back to the poolside lounge for afternoon teas, which involved offering drinks, sandwiches, buttered tea loaf, scones, Madera cake and fresh cream cakes piled high on tiered stands, before going back into the restaurant to begin the evening service for dinners.

By the end of the day my feet were hot and glowing, I felt covered in a lingering smell of food and stale sweat.

The hotel certainly got full value for their 2/6 an hour. It was just nonstop. I dare not take an unauthorised break or keep the tips that were offered by the guests; I was sharply reminded by an eagle-eyed experienced waitress,

"All our tips are shared out at the end of each shift. You're to put yours in too; no matter if anyone says that you are to keep it. Is that clear?"

I just nodded dumbly back at her.

One Sunday evening I was so busy I forgot to fetch the wine to a table until the diners had started on their main course. With horror I realised my mistake and took it over to them.

"No it's far too late now, take it back we don't want it."

I didn't know what to do. The wine had been opened.

"Huh," sniffed one of my colleagues. "That'll have to be taken out of your money today. It'll teach you to be more careful in future."

That evening I had only my tips in my brown envelope to take home; the wine had cost me a day's wages. I don't know what hurt most, the loss of wages or the gloating remarks of the other waitress. They knew that I was at college and perhaps they thought that I needed taking down a peg or two. To be taught a lesson about the 'real world'. And it was an education. It was a world that I had not experienced before in my sheltered, homely, environment. I didn't know how to deflect the sleazy comments from the male guests as I offered them, 'room service Sir!'

"Come on gorgeous, nice bit of room service you've got there."

"I'm all alone here. Worth your while to slip in between my sheets love!"

"Now that's what I call a Full English!"

After a while I got used to the 'variations on a theme' but still didn't know how to reply. They shocked me into silence. I was angry with myself, tongue tied, not knowing what to say without sounding like a little silly frightened girl. I didn't want to be reported for being rude to a guest. I hadn't learnt the art of flippancy and easy humour so that both participants had their pride left in tact. The fact was that I was not street-wise. I blushed too easily and hadn't learnt to deflect the tease with a remark to match theirs. Each time I promised myself that I could control the situation so I fell at the next hurdle.

Even when waiting on at the tables I was shocked at the dismissive attitude of the diners. They would click their fingers impatiently, demand instant attention treating all the waitresses with distain. One dinner time a party of businessmen were becoming more and more rowdy. Several suggestive remarks were made whilst demanding more wine. At the end of their meal I brought the bill as requested and had taken the change back to the table. As they went to leave the dining room I saw that they had taken the silver coin change and substituted one halfpenny in the dish as a 'tip'. I was so angry at their attempt to humiliate me I grabbed the dish without thinking of the consequences and plunged after them.

"Excuse me Sir!" I spoke loudly with exaggerated deference.   "I believe you may have left your change", and placed the half penny into his hand.

The room went quiet. He looked at me as I held his gaze.

I wanted to shout 'don't you dare do that to me' but of course I didn't, but I like to think that he felt the full measure of my anger as I stood, smiling my waitress smile at him, before turning on my heel to dismiss him.

The other waitress had watched the performance. "That's a good customer, you better not've upset him."

But I was beyond caring. Let him complain, for what could he say? That I had given him back some change left in a dish. There was no case to answer. He couldn't report the blaze of anger in my eyes could he?

I turned to her with feigned surprise, "I don't know what you mean".

We left it at that.

It may well have been the 1960's but still there was the legacy of my 1950's upbringing hanging over me. As children we were taught that children should be seen and not heard; that we should do as we were told without questioning the instruction. Young men in the late 1950's had obeyed orders whilst serving their time in the National Service. A doctor's authoritarian diagnosis was never questioned nor was the word of a teacher. If you wanted to know the time 'you asked a policeman,' and hopefully they never gave you a 'thick ear' for any misdemeanour. Those children who played up their parents could be send to the, 'naughty boys' home, or the 'bogey man' might be tempted to take them away. There was an understanding of class, education, age and money; we knew our place and where we stood in the pecking order. As a family we were poor, lived on a council estate, I had been educated at a Secondary Modern school and we had no privileged ancestry. At work you did as you were told or else you 'got your cards'. You toed the line and were grateful for small mercies. Senacre might have provided me with a veneer of confidence but out in the real world I knew that I was on shaky foundations.

During the fourth form at Senacre we visited the 'world of work' to see what job opportunities or subject options we could take up. We visited a bakery up at Parkwood where we saw the same loaves of bread just wrapped in different shop wrappings as each batch was completed. And then we went to a wholesaler's warehouse in Stone Street where we saw them testing the quality of huge rounds of cheese, plunging a long hollow tube into the huge cheese and offering us a piece to try. Fascinating as these visits were I'm not quite sure how relevant the careers advice service was. Later that year I remember we went to a girl's borstal as a part of a visiting netball team. Goodness knows why we did that. We played a fairly abrasive match which I think they probably won, and then were shown around the premises. Many of the hollow-eyed girls had self-harmed and bore shocking deep cut wounds around their wrists. Some were heavily tattooed; the badly drawn, crudely formed hearts and names scrawled across their knuckles or on their bare arms. Even although it was a cold day they seemed oblivious to the biting chill wind as we walked around the green houses and vegetable plots. Some spoke of the 'bleeding judge' who had put them away for 'perjury'.

"If I ad't said it like I was told, me fella would have given me what for an' no mistake."

I realised that they had no choice in their bitter lives. They were damned either way. Some spoke of having to have their own child taken away.

"'e put me up the duff and then buggered off. Dunno where 'e is. Don't want to know either. Last time I saw him 'e broke me nose, said I was on the game. Lousy bastard."

And so I kept my nose clean at the hotel and did the work without complaint. After I had been there a while the senior waitress decided that I could do the large tally sheet which involved a kind of double entry book keeping. All the meals and prices were listed down the left side and then across the top. Manually I had to ensure that the columns and totals at the bottom equated to the tally to the right hand side. It was probably a job that she hated doing. I had one eye on the clock and one eye on the figures desperate to get it right first time as I was fearful of missing the minibus and although I had received some offers for a 'lift home' from some of the male staff I knew full well that that was just looking for trouble.

Meanwhile at college Grahame and I did our best to avoid the sneers of the lecturers. I attempted to follow the 'cobweb theorem' in Economics and the Bear and Bull implications of the stock market but I was seriously out of my depth. I voiced my fears to one of the mature students who was taking the English course.

"I wanted to do English and Art at A level." I said," but they said that I couldn't do that as it wasn't sufficient for a full time course in one year".

"Well that's peculiar!" she looked surprised. "cos that's what I'm doing this year."

I was mortified.

"You should have taken it further you know; gone to the Principal".

But it was all too late. One term was almost over. I was finding it hard to study, and to find time to see Chris. When he came around on a Saturday night after his rugby match I would be repelled to find that he had acquired another set of bruises, a swollen eye or a split lip as a result of a scuffle in the scrum. My life wasn't going in the direction that I had hoped for, but once again I didn't have the courage or energy to redirect it. I had fallen into the relationship without questioning whether I actually wanted it. And how could tell him; that I had grown tired of him, tired of having to play a part?

I sent off an application to a teachers training college in Bingley, in the West Riding of Yorkshire, and received an invitation to have an interview. My success in obtaining a place would be based on the interview and the exam results.

Mum and I went to Cheisemans to buy a suitable interview suit. We finally ended up buying a cerise woollen outfit from Alexon that made me look ten years older than I was. But we thought that it looked the part. I caught the train up to Victoria, London and then across on the underground to Euston. It was the first time that I had made such a journey on my own and I was filled with trepidation and dread that I would miss the train, catch the wrong train, miss the station, or lose the ticket. I anxiously watched as the station names sped past hoping that I didn't have to change anywhere else. The congested tall buildings off London gave way to the smaller rows of houses displaying their private back gardens, sheds and paraphernalia until finally green fields opened up the view, some containing small herds of cows, whilst others were planted with crops. At first I was attentive to it all, pleased to have a window seat and not to have to engage in conversation with anyone. But as the journey went on I realised that I had no idea how far way Yorkshire was from Kent. It had only seemed a small distance when I had looked it up in the road atlas. Finally the fresh fields gave way to tall cooling towers of Sheffield belching out clouds of steam. Then finally, row upon row, of crowded narrow brick houses, back to back, row upon endless row, as far as my eye could see; grey smoke trailing from their chimneys, as Leeds grew ever closer.

I had to change at Leeds and catch another smaller local train to Bingley. Or did I change again at Bradford and then on to Bingley? My memory is hazy, my fear of missing the station jumbled up my thoughts. The college was situated on a hill just a little way up from the town. As I walked in through the front entrance the college grey-stoned building looked grand, suitably old and rather imposing. I had hoped that it would be like that. I didn't expect spires but reassuringly solid was good enough.

The interview didn't take long. Perhaps they liked what they saw; perhaps it was just perfunctory and getting in would merely rest on the results of the exams. I was to stay the night and make the return journey the next morning. The student accommodation on site consisted of four or five large 'halls of residence' set up on a bank at the back of the main building looking down on terraced lawns.

I returned home somewhat discomforted. At the noisy student union bar I had been bluntly asked if I smoked or had had sex. Since I hadn't, but didn't know how to avoid answering, I meekly shrugged and shook my head. Why couldn't I have said something witty and to have laughed off the blatant attempt to embarrass me? But no easy retort came to me.

They nudged each other. "Well tha will do as soon as tha get here!"

The evening did not go well; it was almost a relief to be ignored.

They viewed me as a soft Southerner. Their attempts to make me feel different had succeeded. Stupidly I had, until that evening, no understanding of the North South divide and the deep rooted prejudice. I had no idea that all the decent, 'where tha's muck tha's money', hard working people in the North had been subjugated and oppressed by the idle rich Southerners; that it was agreed that I was 'posh' and privileged' by dint of my southern accent. At first I had thought it was a joke when one student confirmed my status.

"tha'll find it different oop 'ere. Not cosy like y've bin use't."

I stared at him. What on earth did he mean?

Returning home on the train I wondered if I had made another mistake. Perhaps I should have applied closer to home and looked at the courses at Canterbury. I dare not admit my feelings of doubt to Mum and Dad since I had been so stubbornly adamant, arguing about the need to become independent and to apply to a college far away from home. One visit made it obvious that it wasn't just distance that was the problem but that I would be entering another world that didn't treat outsiders with much sympathy. I kept my doubts curled up tight within me and hoped that in time they would disappear.

The demands of everyday drew me back from that reverie, I needed to apply myself to Medway College demands, but then there was a new distraction, and he was beginning to unsettle me. Sitting next to him during the English lessons his hand had accidentally brushed against mine. But when it happened again I realised with a jolt, my stomach contracting and uncurling in a series of waves that he had deliberately sought to caress my fingers.

At the college Christmas dance I danced with Chris. He had not been happy about my application to Bingley and we had argued before the setting out for the dance, having to agree to a reluctant truce before meeting up with Grahame. I had found myself defending a position that I didn't believe in myself, but perhaps part of my need to go away had more to do with him than I was prepared to admit. Perhaps I wanted to escape from his 'happy ever after' plans for us both, rather than my spurious arguments about the college prospectus and being impressed with the ethos that the college presented. Who was I trying to fool?

"If you go away you'll want us to finish." He persisted.

"No I won't. You just don't want me to go to college full stop."

"You'll find some one else."

Perhaps it had already happened. I dare not voice my unease with myself and my reluctance to admit that I had done nothing to discourage the illicit handholding. Why couldn't I be more honest and open why did I lack courage? I didn't want to be with Chris any more. I wasn't excited by him. But I was frightened of his reaction. He would be right. I was shallow and uncaring, for all my superior protestations. I didn't even trust myself.

The music slowed to allow for shuffling couples to smooch. I didn't want to be close to him. His need for me to respond repelled me. The closer he drew me to him the further away I felt. I was being suffocated.

Chris's grip loosened. I became aware that he was no longer dancing cheek to cheek but was staring at someone behind me.

"Am I allowed to ask for a dance with her before the evening is over?"

176

The request, although said lightly with a bemused tone, did not allow for dissention. He had demanded that Chris gave way, and even before Chris had had time to acknowledge his request I found my face pressed against Terry's chest, one hand tightly gripping mine whilst his other hand placed on the small of my back drew me firmly towards him. I became engulfed in a powerful dose of Brut aftershave. My heart thumped against my chest. I could feel the passion of his embrace as we swayed to the music.

Then all too soon the dance was over. I was returned to my partner, nothing was said. Only my hands, still slightly clammy, were evidence that something different had happened. I wiped them down the sides of my dress; wiping away my guilty pleasure.

One dance, what did it signify? He had not even spoken to me as we danced. I was thrilled by him. That he had chosen to wait so far into the evening before asking to dance. It was a statement of intention. I am here. I will be seeing you again. Chris was quiet during the journey home; we hardly spoke.

The following Saturday we went to the ten-pin bowling alley in Chatham. On the return journey to Maidstone Chris drove through the town and then turned up Stone Street. He recklessly attempted to pass a bus at speed. I could see that the central reservation did not allow space for two vehicles. He put his foot down to avoid the bus but we simultaneously hit both the side of the bus and the kerb of the reservation with a scream of metal as we came to a shuddering stop.

Once the recriminations between the drivers were over and the details of insurance had been given, the car limped back home. Our lives are like this I thought. I am between two forces and they will crush me. I can't go on as we are; I need to finish this confusion and stop the anger and frustration that is eating him up. But I said and did nothing.

Some afternoons after college I would gaze into Cornell's window in Gabriel's' Hill hungrily eyeing the trays of gleaming rings set with sapphires, rubies, emeralds and the exquisite mystery of milky opals swirling in subtle hues of blues, reds and greens, ever changing as the light caught them. On impulse I bought some cheap gold coloured earrings from Dunnings in Week Street. The clip earrings had a long rod, at the bottom of which hung a fashioned rose. I was thrilled with them.

"When you go to San Francisco be sure to wear some flowers in your hair."

I now wore flowers, and crooning the song met Grahame at the bus stop to catch the bus to college. We raced up the stairs to settle at our favourite seats.

"Well," I said shaking my head to make the earrings shiver, "what do you think of them?"

"Of what?" he appeared confused.

"My earrings of course!" I turned my head to free them from my long hair and to show them in a better light

"Well," I think it would have been better if you had bought two."

"Two!" My hands went to both ears. It was true; I only had one earring. "Oh no I must have just lost it." We scrabbled around searching the floor under the seat, but to on avail.

"And I've hardly had them on for two minutes." I was cross, but then on seeing Grahame's face dissolve as he attempted not to laugh meant that we both ended up roaring with laughter.

"And how do you like my new earrings," he mimicked me, flashing his eyes and girlishly shaking his head, which set us off once again.

Through out the journey I had only to look at him, as he fluffed his hand by the side of his head as if to display an earring, and it would have us convulsed once again, helpless with laughter; the type of rib aching, painful laughter that used to occur in church when you practically had to stuff your mouth with a handkerchief to stop the giggling infection from spreading.

I had to force myself to concentrate on the flashing scenery gazing from the window as the ticket inspector came up the stairs to check our tickets and snip a corner in it before descending.

When it came to companionship, Grahame was second to none. We always found something to cheer ourselves up on those journeys back and forth from Chatham. Even when the college lecturers had been particularly unpleasant and the remarks on our essays unforgiving we managed to be in good humour by the time Maidstone came into view.

One day the older of the two English lecturers had ranted on about homosexuality whilst we were looking at passages of text from James Joyce's 'A portrait of an Artist as a Young Man' He believed that 'every one of them should be put up against a wall and shot'. We were horrified, first by his outburst, and then by the strength of his raw, ugly anger. He held his pipe in his withered hand, attempting to stuff tobacco inside it as we looked at each other not knowing how to respond. Where had so much pent up aggression come from? Had he been so incensed by the recent Government Act to decriminalise homosexuality and needed to get things off his chest? But no discussion was forthcoming; his anger stopped us from challenging him.

I was becoming more and more at odds with Dad at home, challenging his views instead of the easy acceptance that had featured during our long chats after a meal. The commentators had condemned Enoch Powell and his warnings about 'rivers of blood'. Dad was incensed by the outcry that ensued.

"You mark my words, in time to come they'll have to say that he was right." Then it will be too late for the poor bugger. People don't know what they are talking about. Never been anywhere to find out either."

"But discrimination is wrong! He is making people scared."

"And so they should be. The country is too full as it is."

"But........"

"Living ten to a room"

"That's not how...."

"And dressed in fancy suits; when have I owned just one suit. How do they afford that huh?"

"So now they shouldn't be smart!"

"No wonder the pound has gone down the drain."

"That's got noting to do with it!"

"No? If it's not the blacks or Asians coming here then it's the French telling us what to do. Charles Bloody De Gaulle, happy to be here during the war wasn't he?.... then had to sneak back home when the coast was clear.....and now telling us who and who can't join the European Common Market. If it wasn't for us there wouldn't be a Europe at all."

The argument raged crazily from one topic to another as we battled to make our point. How was it that my arguments sounded so good in my head but once I started to voice them they seemed to dissipate and float away?

I continued to bury myself in my books. The lending library at the 'top shops' still provided most of them. My taste changed according to what was on offer. I sobbed under the bedclothes reading 'Gone with the Wind', grabbed all the John Steinbeck novels and Neville Shute, John Wyndham, John Braine, Thomas Hardy, HE Bates, Ernest Hemmingway, James Joyce and DH Lawrence. It wasn't until I finally went away to college that I met the 19th century writers of Dickens, Austin, Wilkie Collins, Elliott, Mrs Gaskell, the French authors Zola, Flaubert's Madame Bovary, and Balzac, the Russians, Dostoyevsky, Tolstoy, and Chechov, and the 19th and 20th century Americans, Edith Wharton and Bellow; spending the best part of my grant on books.

At home we still had no television and relied on our vists to Gran to catch up on the popular programmes of Dad's Army, the Antique Road Show, and the new satirical That Was the Week that Was.

During that year Linda and I decided to take an 'O' level Geography at evening classes, thinking that it might boost our chances to get into college. I was so tired at the end of the day and regularly used to find myself almost nodding off during the lesson. It was no wonder that I failed the exam. The teacher set us a few test examples. One was to explain how sand dunes were formed. I was totally perplexed. How indeed! My answer? That sand banked up around a dead camel and eventually the sand hill got bigger and bigger as the wind blew against it. I don't think he was impressed. Nor did he find it amusing when I wrote that a winding river would eventually form an 'ox-tail' lake. A red biro in the margin declared 'ox-bow!' and I believe my score out of twenty was approximately a two.

My Sundays at the Great Danes were easier once the warmer weather came. It was nice not having to get up in the dark, and not having to start the day by freezing whilst waiting for the minibus to arrive. The waitresses had more or less accepted me by then and I had learnt to ignore the chefs and their tantrums. I also had been relieved of doing the room service breakfasts to business guests as they had more families staying on holiday who appeared to want to eat in the main dining room before starting their day, so I waited at the tables straight away. Whilst the morning was easier, the poolside restaurant became busier. The families took their young children to the pool so there was a constant clamour for mid-morning coffees, soft drinks, crisps, scones and cakes. My tips at the end of the day easily surpassed the amount that I received in wages and allowed me to buy a couple of bits and pieces in town, besides paying for my weekly fare to Chatham.

I had had a little family 'do' at home for my eighteenth birthday and had unexpectedly received a dainty rolled-gold watch Avia from Mum and Dad. I was thrilled with it. In my small shell-covered jewellery box I now gloated over my collection of treasures. A thin rolled gold slightly bent Christening bracelet, a small gold Christening brooch with my name etched in copperplate, and a small gold signet ring. Then there was a yellow and green beaded necklace from the Sunday school, a few enamelled golliwog badges, a school prefect badge, a Senacre pin that Dad had fashioned from a piece of brass. Finally there was a silver St Christopher with a very thin chain that I had found on the day trip to Calais all those years ago. Oh yes, and one golden earring with a rose hanging from the long gold rod.

I coveted the small amount of 1940's style costume jewellery that Mum had. A delicate brooch of flowers, daises and cornflowers counted as one of my favourites. If Heather had gone in for jewellery I never saw it. She kept it well away from my prying eyes. She had produced some small blue and white pots and vases that she had made whilst at college, and two bowls, one each for Mum and Dad which sat on the windowsill alongside the brass housefly and the small brass cannon. We had few ornaments in those days apart from a small pair of wooden elephant heads with white tusks that Dad had brought back from Egypt and some trinket dishes that contained copious amounts of pins, paperclips, buttons, small screws and other useless bits that never found a proper home but couldn't be thrown away in case they were needed.

On Mum's dressing table sat another piece that I coveted. A small glass hare sat on its hind legs, its elongated ears ready to hold some rings for its owner, covered in a fine layer of face powder that had escaped from a glass jar.

Downstairs in the kitchen it was another similar story. Mum's top drawer was stuffed with old ration books, a battered and well-used cookery book, recipes torn out from magazines, old and current paying in books for the Prudential man. Then there were bits of curled up string, a couple of dusty sticks of burgundy sealing wax, out of date coupons for numerous food items, paper clips, drawing pins, matches, a battered tin containing needles for a gramophone that we did not possess. She had kept an old wheel shaped pen and pencil eraser that had last seen service when she had been working as a shorthand typist before she met Dad and there was a motley collection of pencil stubs, pens and biros that didn't work. A well-used pair of scissors managed to find themselves a convenient space amongst the jumble alongside some rolls of sellotape slightly grubby around the edges, and a pair of slightly rusty tweezers.

"It's more like a nest than a drawer," Dad teased her. Just as she was haphazard in her approach to storage so he was tidy and neat. But they both had the squirrel mentality of the 1930's and 1940's and couldn't bear to throw anything away that could possibly be used for another purpose. Old knickers and worn out torn vests became our dusters or floor cloths and other useless paraphernalia took up residence until they were called upon to perform some duty.

In the bottom kitchen drawer Dad kept his handy house tools, screwdrivers, a hammer, a couple of metal files, a few pair of pliers, various nuts and bolts, spare batteries and a heavy duty torch. He had some sand paper of various grades, his decorating brushes were kept cleaned with white spirit, spare light bulbs and everything could be produced on demand.

Although we teased Mum about her collections of rubbish she still felt no compulsion to change her ways. As soon as any storage space became available so she managed commandeer it. In the front room she kept her sewing box, and a various selection of tins. An old Coronation tin celebrating Victoria and Albert housed a collection of assorted buttons. Some tins were stuffed with steel pins, others more buttons, and then there was a bag of knitting needles, some crochet needles and cards of thick darning wool with a large wooden mushroom shaped darning dome. A leather Crinoline Lady shaped needle case kept a variety of fine needles amongst her layered skirts trailing end threads of previously used cottons. And then there was a pair of sewing scissors and numerous Coats Cotton wooden reels haphazardly scattered in an old green metal box, its battered hinges denoting that it had once possessed a lid. The cottons had become intertwined which each other so that before a project could begin they all had to be untangled from each other. Since there were various tins stuffed with buttons I asked Mum why there were so many buttons; some gold ones decorated with an anchor appeared to have been snipped off Dad's naval uniform.

She shrugged, "I think that when I was pregnant with Heather I used to do it", she shook her head. "I can't think why!"

Perhaps as the time approached for me to leave home I started to become nostalgic about a childhood that was about to end. But I didn't allow myself to voice the doubts about the path that I had chosen. I was still too determined to prove that I could succeed despite the failures of the past. I wanted to go into teaching because I had witnessed at first hand how an inspired teacher makes a difference but whether I had the ability to inspire I didn't like to consider. I was too busy wanting some recognition, ambition and vanity drove me on. And what was the alternative? I had no secretarial training didn't want to nurse or be a librarian, or work in a bank, nor did I have the art skills to become a commercial artist like Heather. I didn't even consider those things that consumed me with a passion, a love of animals, the countryside, the flora and fauna around me and a talent for cutting hair!

Somehow it was something that I started to do. Cutting Dad's hair and getting a half-crown for my efforts. His hair circled an ever-growing bald patch.

"If I go to the barbers they will have to charge a search fee!" He never failed to make me giggle.

So what talents and abilities did I inherit from my ancestors? Dad was poetic, personifying nature. His love letters to Mum written during their courtship and marriage whilst he was away at sea resonated with his love of the English countryside, the colours of autumn and the softly falling rain renewing the land and his dreams of being at home with her. He was a craftsman, an engineer, an artist, a compete Renaissance man. In his hands tools responded to his touch. Even when painting a door his brush and he became as one. His dexterity charmed me. I delighted in his ability to create and his tenacity in overcoming an obstacle.

Mum, despite her aversion to order and housework was an emotional homemaker. She created a haven of non-judgmental safety and unconditional love even when her patience was tested to the limit. She was always at hand to care; had a hot water bottle at the ready when the monthly pains became too much, offered a cup of tea when she thought that you must be thirsty, did the washing up after cooking a meal and never complained when we thoughtlessly didn't offer to help. But unlike Dad she was completely cack-handed.

"If there's a wrong way to do something Joy'll find it!" He teased her affectionately.

So was I the sum of those two halves or were there older claims on my persona? Dad's maternal grandfather had been a head gardener working on large estates in Norfolk and Kent, did I inherit a passion for plants from him? Then there was my Mum's grandfather, a gent's hairdresser with his own business in Stone Street. Did I inherit a knack of cutting hair from him? And my pride and ambition, was that from the Payne side of the family?

We had learnt of Dad's painful history when Heather had the urge to create a family tree. Dad brought out a small battered wood veneered box which contained all his childhood and history. A little key turned the lock. Inside the separate compartments he drew out scraps of paper, a few chess pieces, some medals, a golden sovereign along with some old tiny silver sixpences and a few old Victorian pennies. Then a faded picture emerged of a young girl, sitting, looking towards the camera, her little booties, just visible, beneath her Victorian styled skirt.

"That's my real Mum, Dorothy Rose", he fingered the picture carefully.

Heather and I were astounded. His real mother! But what of Christie in Nottingham and miserable Father Payne?

"The old fella made her pregnant after he had married her sister." He said bitterly.

She died when I was three,...... I never knew her."

"But Sally, is she still your sister?"

"My half sister. And then there's Tom."

"Your brother?"

"Nope...........he's my nephew."

He began the sorry tale of his grandfather May, the head gardener and his wife who eventually came to live in Cranbrook. They had three daughters and a son confusingly also named Amos like our Dad and the grandfather was our Aunty Joan's father. Uncle Amos was a favourite with Dad and so he used to come down from Nottingham and stay with him. And that's how he met Mum because; she and his cousin Joan were school friends.

He continued the story. The oldest girl, Charlotte Mary, called Lottie by her family had had a child out of wedlock in 1909 and had died the following year. Chrissie, whom we had always thought of as Dad's mother, was Christiana and had given birth to just one child, our Aunty Sally, in 1915. Dorothy Rose had been made pregnant by Chrissie's husband Herbert and given birth to our Dad in 1920. Dad had been whisked away to live with Chrissie and Herbert and poor Dorothy Rose, lost her child and was left behind in Kent. She died in 1923, and so Dad had no childhood memory of her.

"So why did you say that Tom is your nephew?"

"Well the old man and Chrissie took in a lodger to get some extra money and he made Sally pregnant. Sally had Tom when she was just fourteen. But my poor old Mum, Chrissie took him on as her own."

We could see how much Chrissie meant to Dad, and the anger he felt towards Herbert his father.

"He had a nasty temper when I was a kid. If we played chess and he thought that he was going to lose, he used to snap the board shut and all the pieces would shower over the floor!"

Dad had taught me to play chess years before but my memories of being taught to play consisted of his delight when he thought that I had started to improve and his immense pleasure when I finally managed to take a game from him. So different from his experience! And he promised that if I continued to improve he would carve a chess set for me.

Dad had ensured that our upbringing reflected none of the anger and brutality of his own childhood.

"The old man drank like a fish. He never had money in the house. Poor Chrissie had to manage on the pittance that he allowed her for housekeeping and food. She never saw his wage packet."

No wonder Dad handed over his brown wage packet to Mum after having deducted his 'baccy' money. It was to demonstrate his aversion to everything that his own father had stood for. Was that why he never drank, that he was teetotal?

"If there was an egg in the house for breakfast, we kids would never have it. He would eat it in front of us." The hurt of his youth spilled out.

Mum nodded. She had known how it had been for him. Her childhood with a loving father had been so different.

"And this box is all I have to show for it." He turned out scraps of paper with the words 'Dorothy Rose' written in ink by a child's hand.

"My real Mum had something wrong with her spine, ... don't think she could walk very well .... spent a lot of time in a wheelchair so I was told."

"When I got home from the war I found that the old man had thrown everything out of mine. This was all that I could salvage." His hurt was evident, still raw all through the years it had followed him.

There were hints of violence towards Chrissie. I realised that Dad, despite all the rows and shouting had never raised his hand to us. His relationship with Mum had at times been fraught, just silly tiffs, nothing that lingered, but his care towards us, playing with us spending so much time with us had given us the security and care that he had never experienced with his own father. Why was it that in some families the same mistakes were repeated and yet for us Dad provided a different pattern to shape us? Was it Mum's gentle care early on in their relationship that allowed him to show this side of his personality?

And so whom did I take after? Mum said that I reminded her of her father. And yet I had a quick temper; would hold long term, unforgiving grudges, and be so difficult at times. Her father was placid and patient. I was certainly not patient. Always too impatient and that had been a problem for far too long. To watch Heather slowly unpick some embroidery since a stitch seemed less than perfect filled me with frustration. And to see Dad go, "back to the drawing board!" to begin all over again, irrationally irritated me. Yes I suppose I had inherited some artistic talent, could move to music like Dad, enjoyed singing and could hold a tune. Now where did that come from? Dad's father Herbert could play the violin and the mandolin, Dad played the piano but could not read music. I was practical, could see how to put things together and was beginning to appreciated order and tidiness in the house.

"If a job's worth doing it's worth doing well" was a mantra that I could relate to. And yet if someone had said 'I want to climb the north face of the Eiger, just because it is there, to see if I can reach the summit' I would have thought him or her mad. Why not see if the south side is an easier way to get up! Hardship for hardship's sake was an anathema to me. I celebrated finding a quick and easy solution that, to me, defined intelligence! I wanted to master a problem not create one. That a true artist would ensure that the unseen face of a sculpture would be as perfect as the front was something that I could respect but not understand. Why spend time doing something that would never ever be appreciated?

Unfortunately I had to acknowledge that I was also vain. Vanity, and the thought of how others viewed me drove me on when I would have otherwise have lacked the will to continue. Neither Dad nor Mum I considered as being vain. Mum could be a snob, but then so could I, just for different reasons, and perhaps more devious in hiding it.

Mum was always keen to tell us about her maternal great -grandfather Porter who had been something very important in the City of London, 'as he always went up to London wearing a top hat'. She thought that, at least, he was a postmaster. In later years when I had researched the family history it was with a sense of betrayal when I discovered that his occupation on the census form was as a postman. She also had a few family photographs of the two Porter sisters expensively dressed in tucked and pinned Victorian dress, their hair pinned up leaving a few curls to fashionably cascade down in elaborate ringlets.

"They were obviously well-to-do as both Louise and Addie had piano lessons."

I head the story so many times. Our well-heeled family had mysteriously lost their fortune somewhere along the way. And then of course was the Burley side of the family on her grandfather's side. His Sheffield family had worked with silver. Gran still had some family pieces on her sideboard. And Grandfather Burley had a successful hairdressing business in Stone Street that had enabled him to buy one of his sons a sweet shop and also ensured that the two sons were able to be financially secure. The story seemed at odds with the fact that Gran, his daughter had been put to work as a maid in a big house in London before she met her gentle William Kempshall.

The time to leave home was fast approaching. My relationship with Chris was waning. I knew that I needed to revise for the exams but kept prevaricating. Tomorrow, I promised myself. Tomorrow I will knuckle down to it. When the sun was shining it was too nice to be inside. When it was too cold, then it was too cold to concentrate. There were a number of excuses that I could conjure up. Just as I had done on my way to school when I was just eight or nine. I would hurry up the road towards the junior school trying to remember what excuse for being late that I had provided the day before. The alarm clock had broken. The cat was sick. The back door key was lost and I had to spend time looking for it. No marks for originality and totally unconvincing, even to me at the time and yet I never learnt to be allow the proper amount of time to get there. What was I doing that made me so late? I have no idea. It wasn't about getting up; I was a lark rather than an owl so found it easy to rise each morning.

But now the term was coming to an end and I knew that I was running out of time to make adequate provision for studying. Grahame came round to help us both revise but his company was so enjoyable that we ended up spending time chatting rather than concentrating on the work. He was like the brother that I had always craved. He had applied for a college in Dudley and Linda had applied for one in Coventry. Within a few months our chosen paths would separate us from our childhood and our past.

If I was successful in obtaining a place at Bingley College we had to apply for a grant that was available for low-income families. We were eligible. The means tested grant took all income into consideration, so Mum domestic work had to be included in the assessment. We also had to apply for travel expenses. I knew that Mum and Dad would find it hard to afford to fund any unexpected expenses and so I realised that I needed to get some savings together before I went up to Yorkshire.

Linda and I decided that we could get a six-week summer job in a Holiday Camp. There had been vacancies and they appeared to pay well, board and lodging included. I traitorously applied before telling Mum and Dad. They were horrified when they found out what I had done.

"We will be losing you for three years as it is and now you want to leave home sooner than that!"

They were right. I couldn't explain it myself. What was the pressing need to leave, when, in my heart of hearts I didn't want to leave home? My home had become, if anything, dearer to me now that I knew that I was no longer going to be living there. It was quite irrational. Surely I could have found some employment in Maidstone. Or was it that I need to prove to myself that I was brave enough to be

189

independent and this was a way of breaking myself in? Was it that as Linda had seen the advert, and I had vaguely, without thinking, agreed to commit to the idea then suddenly, when the application had arrived, couldn't lose face? All cowardly whichever way it was. Symptomatic of my approach to so many aspects of my life.

The exams came and went. I knew that I wasn't going to pass the Economics 'A' level. The paper threw me into a panic of hot confusion as I read over the incomprehensible questions. That I even managed to acquire an 'O' level pass was quite remarkable, as I had no idea about the correct responses that were required. I tried to fill the paper with snippets of understanding desperately hoping that they would gain a few marks.

But I was confident with the 'A' level English paper. I knew the texts well and hoped that my answers agreed with the examiners brief. Grahame and I had seen the new musical 'Canterbury Tales earlier that year and it had helped to put the flesh on the bones of the characters.

With the exams over our time at Medway College ended. Linda and I set off for the holiday camp. I was to be a chalet maid and she was to work at the refreshment kiosks. My paper said that I would be paid £6.10 with free living accommodation. After the first week we queued up for our week's payment and on opening my wage packet found that I only had £6.00 I went back to the cashier at the desk.

"I only have £6.00 here." I showed her the slip accompanying the notes. "I should have been paid £6.10."

"No," the weekly rate for a chalet maid is £6.00." She peered at me above her glasses having in her mind dismissed me, wondering why I still hadn't left.

But I could feel a sense of injustice rising, and attempted to keep calm.

"My letter of employment says that I will be paid £6.10 for a weeks work."

She sighed. "We pay £6.10 for other types of work, but a chalet maid gets £6.00" She attempted to get back to her paper work.

"My letter is a contact of employment." I persisted. "To pay me less would be breaking that contract."

She jerked upright. "Show me the letter!" she demanded.

I produced it.

She scanned the contents. "The amount that has been put in here is purely a typing error."

"It may be, but it is still a contract, which is legally binding." I had no idea whether it was or not but had nothing to lose.

She looked again at me sharply as seeing me for the first time. There were others behind me who were also awaiting the outcome of the argument. I could almost physically feel their interest growing.

"Well, purely as a matter of goodwill we will agree to it, but only as a goodwill gesture." She sneered.

"That's fine by me." I walked away triumphantly. I had won the day! For once my courage had not failed me.

The weeks at the holiday camp were salutary reminders of how others lives were lived. For some workers who were there for the season, the transitory companionship of their fellow workers was the only relationships that they had. During that summer we had floods that overwhelmed the chalets, covering the area in knee deep mud. A child noticed an unmoving swimmer at the bottom of the pool and after several attempts to gain the life guard's attention he found that it was too late; that the man had suffered a heart attack and drowned. Then there was the tyre-slashing episode when some youths had managed to penetrate the fences or had slipped in through the gates and had slit the tyres of the cars parked in the car park.

I was glad to get home.

There were only a few days left before I had to leave. Dad had arranged to take me up to London in his car and see me off at Euston station. Leaving home was going to be harder than I thought it would be. Suddenly so many features of home became so important that had been merely mundane in the past. I peeped into Dad's workshop. His well oiled tools, his pots and jars, and lathe, curls of metal on the bench and half-finished Black Five loco all seemed to reproach me. Hadn't we had fun here? Why are you going?

I wandered around the garden. Who would tend my vegetable patch? Our cat followed my progress up the path. I gazed at the small weeded strawberry patch, then the site of an old bonfire, and the raspberry canes towards the end of the pathway. Since I had worked the garden the soil had improved yielding to my fork. We had had a bumper crop of strawberries that year. I had even managed to contain the bindweed, although it was always ready to emerge from under the pathway, hiding with the industrious red ants that persisted in making their nest just by the small rockery where the soil was sandier. Many times I had had to disturb them when trying to eradicate the bindweed and then watched them as they frantically carried their large white lava away from the terrible destruction that I had caused.

"I wish that you would make your nest somewhere else," I told them, but they were far too busy to hear.

Mum clattered about in her kitchen, the comforting familiar smell of her lamb stew wafting towards me. I could feel my throat constricting uncomfortably.

It started to rain hard during the night. By the morning the dark clouds swept across the sky. A small puddle had formed at the far kerbside when I first looked out and by the time that I had washed and dressed it had covered the road. The bend of the road had become a lake. Dad had already left for work.

On the far side of Mote Park in a small field two horses were becoming restless. They had trotted to one side where the grass was not so sodden. The unrelenting downpour bounced off their shinning flanks. One started to whinny nervously. They both shook their manes, nuzzled up to each other and shook, sending out arcs of water. Beneath their hooves the mud churned as they pressed against the fence. In the park the trees had become grey shadows, hardly distinguishable through the torrential sheets of rain.

By now the horses were becoming frantic as the dark water swirled around their legs. Plunging their heads up and down their desperate neighing seemed lost in the roar of rain and water. At the side gate of the field a bedraggled figure groped her way, struggling with the sodden rope that held the gate shut. The two horses turned towards her. Between the girl and them raged a rising lake. They hesitated as they heard her call. They both started to move towards her but then feeling the deeper water beneath them retreated again back to the higher ground by the fence. She called more urgently to them coaxing them to come to her, the gate wide open. The horse reared up and as if suddenly galvanised into action plunged through the water towards her, kicking up waves of muddy swirls in its wake. The second horse took a second or two before it too followed on ploughing through the water, it too creating eddy currents as they both galloped through the gate with her.

Down at Turkey Mill the water had risen, it had already flooded the lower buildings. A mill worker hurried away from the submerged buildings towards the arches to reach the Ashford Road on higher ground passing Dad's parked car. He heard a roar and on looking up saw a wave of water coming towards him. He was transfixed. There was nowhere to escape. The only exit was enveloped in the mountain of water that was bearing down on him. As the force of he water hit him he was bounced against the mill wall, hitting his head against the brickwork.

His body was recovered later. Dad's car was also pulled from the water a few days later.

In Maidstone town the small River Len, a small subsidiary to the River Medway, had broken its banks, flooded the Granada cinema and continued to surge along Knightrider Street, submerge the old Coach Museum and the Bishop's Palace which was positioned on the opposite side of the road. It triumphantly poured across the road to join the vastly swelling roaring black lake of the River Medway. The arches of the Medway Bridge were just visible as large branches of trees and tangled rubbish caught underneath forcing the water surge and foam through them.

Maidstone High Street was just visible at the top end where the monument of young Victoria stood imperiously in her sheltered stone Rotunda, facing away from rising water. The water had foreshortened shops at the lower end of the High Street, their lower windows beneath the rushing water.

And so it continued to rain.

From my bedroom window I glanced out looking towards Mote Park. Instead of seeing the green pastureland, all I could see was a grey lake through the rain. The water on our road had started to cover the pathway outside our front gate. How far would the water rise? It had already poured down the little lane opposite that led down the Keepers cottage in the park. But despite the rain's best endeavours the lake didn't encroach up our path. Our house, cut off from the road remained high and dry. My worst nightmare was not realised. Eventually the waters receded. In the Kent Messenger, we read the stories and looked at the pictures taken of our 1968 flood, scenes of the town under water dominating the news.

Dad had to have his car towed to the garage to have it repaired. And as for him taking me to London to assist me on part of my journey to college, that was now out of the question. I was to leave home unaccompanied.

Perhaps independence hard won tastes sweeter. Mine seemed a bitter pill to swallow. I knew that I was fulfilling a dream for Dad. He was thrilled to know that his daughter was one step closer in entering the professional class, just as he was proud to see Heather succeed in her chosen field. Ah, but that was the difference. Had I a vocation for teaching, was this my chosen field? How much had my path been chosen for me? I had fully embraced the modern thinking of equality for women, that somehow the idea of setting up home and having children was an anathema; that now educated women could chose their destiny and not be drowned in a sea of domesticity. At long last the availability of the pill was allowing women to choose a reliable method of contraception, and due to the parliamentary act legalising abortion, women were no longer condemned to an unwanted or unplanned pregnancy. Even the word 'domesticity' was derisory to my ears, for I had a career planned.

For that's what I told myself. I was living in an age of protest. The ruling classes would get their comeuppance. Inherited wealth bad; working classes good. For I had read 'Animal Farm' and 'The Ragged Trousered Philanthropist', and '1984', so had I not understood the messages? French students in Paris would lead the way to resisting the status quo that needed to be torn down. We were going to become angry young men and women and change the world. But was it my war? My indoctrination had been so subtle that I hadn't even noticed it.

I argued that the old British Empire was lamentable, that Apartheid was wrong, segregation was dehumanising, that our English history was littered with such shameful acts of aggression that made every other empire's acts pale into insignificance. Our oppressive nation had created slaves and martyrs. Our industrialised age had been forged from the subjugation of the masses. Those in power were accountable. There needed to be solidarity, equality, freedom from poverty, and opportunity for all. I did not consider those who had enterprise, initiative or an entrepreneurial spirit to be celebrated; they were part of the problem not the solution. Religion was the opium of the people. Things were never as clear as they were back then; so black and white and easily defined. I knew everything about anything, except about myself.

But I still required one established institution despite being sympathetic to the ideals of anarchy and not really getting the 'without rulers could result in lawlessness and chaos' bit. Mum and I went down the town to open a current account with the National Westminster Bank, to pay in my grant that I would receive each term, together with a small amount of money that I had managed to save from the holiday camp work. I bought a long black and white mac with a fashionable animal print from Featherstone's and a pair of long knee length leather boots. My student disguise; would I recognise myself? From somewhere we also bought a chest for my clothes and belongings that was to travel up to Yorkshire separately.

And that was about it. The preparations had all been made. All that remained was just a ticket to purchase for the journey and that was it. Everything had been packed; ego intact, but a heart in tatters. At Oxford Road the tearful goodbyes had been said.

Promises to write.

Last check. Money? Ticket?

Yes, its here!

Then everything suddenly happens far, far, way too fast. A seat is found; my heavy case is lugged aboard and sits alongside me. The train pulls away from the station. There is only just time to wave once more before the one forlorn figure on the platform disappears, snatched away. The train curves away from the station dragging me away from family and home. I am on my own now. No going back. What have I done?

Goodbye!

Left: Linda and I complete the 44 mile overnight walk for the Cheshire Homes charity

Below: Heather took me to see Joan Baez. The original programme from 1967 priced two shillings and sixpence. The 1968 Hair programme from the show that I also saw at the Shaftsbury Theatre in London.

Top: Heather with Dad and then Mum and Dad in the late sixties
Bottom: Me in the summer of 1968.

Standard Pedigree Tree

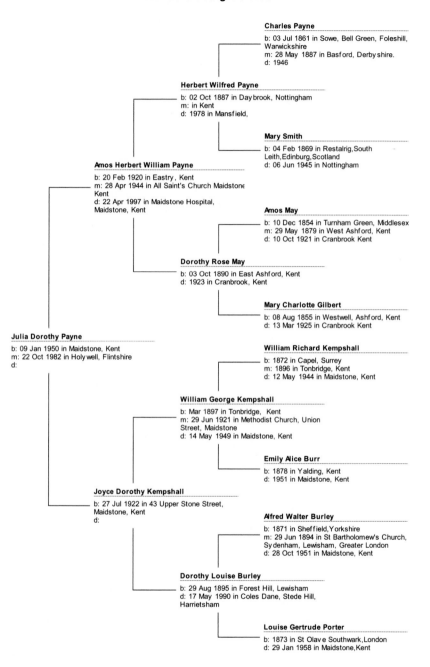

Charles Payne
b: 03 Jul 1861 in Sowe, Bell Green, Foleshill, Warwickshire
m: 28 May 1887 in Basford, Derbyshire.
d: 1946

Herbert Wilfred Payne
b: 02 Oct 1887 in Daybrook, Nottingham
m: in Kent
d: 1978 in Mansfield,

Mary Smith
b: 04 Feb 1869 in Restalrig, South Leith, Edinburg, Scotland
d: 06 Jun 1945 in Nottingham

Amos Herbert William Payne
b: 20 Feb 1920 in Eastry, Kent
m: 28 Apr 1944 in All Saint's Church Maidstone Kent
d: 22 Apr 1997 in Maidstone Hospital, Maidstone, Kent

Amos May
b: 10 Dec 1854 in Turnham Green, Middlesex
m: 29 May 1879 in West Ashford, Kent
d: 10 Oct 1921 in Cranbrook Kent

Dorothy Rose May
b: 03 Oct 1890 in East Ashford, Kent
d: 1923 in Cranbrook, Kent

Mary Charlotte Gilbert
b: 08 Aug 1855 in Westwell, Ashford, Kent
d: 13 Mar 1925 in Cranbrook Kent

Julia Dorothy Payne
b: 09 Jan 1950 in Maidstone, Kent
m: 22 Oct 1982 in Holywell, Flintshire
d:

William Richard Kempshall
b: 1872 in Capel, Surrey
m: 1896 in Tonbridge, Kent
d: 12 May 1944 in Maidstone, Kent

William George Kempshall
b: Mar 1897 in Tonbridge, Kent
m: 29 Jun 1921 in Methodist Church, Union Street, Maidstone
d: 14 May 1949 in Maidstone, Kent

Emily Alice Burr
b: 1878 in Yalding, Kent
d: 1951 in Maidstone, Kent

Joyce Dorothy Kempshall
b: 27 Jul 1922 in 43 Upper Stone Street, Maidstone, Kent
d:

Alfred Walter Burley
b: 1871 in Sheffield, Yorkshire
m: 29 Jun 1894 in St Bartholomew's Church, Sydenham, Lewisham, Greater London
d: 28 Oct 1951 in Maidstone, Kent

Dorothy Louise Burley
b: 29 Aug 1895 in Forest Hill, Lewisham
d: 17 May 1990 in Coles Dane, Stede Hill, Harrietsham

Louise Gertrude Porter
b: 1873 in St Olave Southwark, London
d: 29 Jan 1958 in Maidstone, Kent

Notes:

199

Top left: Dad's parents, Herbert and Dorothy Rose. *Top right*: Mum's family. *Middle:* Amos and Joyce's wedding 1944, Dad's sister Sally on his left and Mum's sister Betty on her right. *Bottom*: Heather and Julia